WHAT PEOPLE AR
DEFINING DE

MW01032099

As a new Christian, I spent nearly a decade in the Mystical-Miracle Move-ment. I saw firsthand the false teachings, deception, and harm that this movement has wrought. I am very grateful that Costi Hinn and Anthony Wood have written this work, exposing the teachers and teachings of the Mystical-Miracle movement. What they say is spot on! In a day when the church's discernment is at a historical low, this book is much needed.

Dr. Michael Vlach
Professor of Theology, The Master's Seminary, Sun Valley, California

The truth has hard edges. Even when two caring shepherds speak it in love, sometimes it still stings. For those who are quick to high-five any who say 'I love Jesus' a book like this may be an uncomfortable read. But it's important. *Defining Deception* will do the crucial work of tracing the background, identifying the key players, and explaining the damage that the latest wave of sign-seeking is doing to the Christ's Church. Hinn and Wood have provided a valuable resource in this timely work. I encourage you get a copy for yourself and for any you know who are being lured into this so-called "Apostolic Reformation."

Dr. Mike Fabarez
Pastor of Compass Bible Church, Aliso Viejo, California

I was reared in the Pentecostal-Charismatic movement. I came to a knowledge of Jesus and basic Bible truths through the teaching of my parents, and godly teachers in my church. But not all Pentecostals and Charismatic share the same emphases. The authors of *Defining Deception: Freeing the Church from the Mystical-Miracle Movement* take care to distinguish standard Pentecostalism from the extreme miracle movements of Word-Faith and Third Wave Charismatic movements. Whereas historic Pentecostalism, for the most part, has adhered to orthodox Christianity, new Charismatic preachers and churches often deviate from the Bible in the teachings regarding the biblical doctrines of revelation, God, Jesus, and salvation. Leaders of the Word-Faith Movement and the Third Wave tend to emphasize subjective experience, rather than theology, money rather than people, and deceit rather than transparency. Hinn and Wood carefully and irenically expose false teachers and false doctrines and deceptive methods, but with due concern for accuracy and thoroughness, and explain well the difference between the nature of biblical miracles with the tricks and illusions of the "signs and wonders" teaching and teachers. This book will help persons who find themselves in the "miracles" movement, and provide a rationale for them to develop a more biblical teaching on miracles and relationship with Jesus.

Dr. H. (Hershel) Wayne House
Vice-President of Academic Affairs and Distinguished Professor of Theology, Law, and Culture, Faith International University, Faith Seminary, Tacoma, Washington

I'm sure *Defining Deception* was not an easy book for the authors to write. It's never easy to expose error without doing so in brush strokes that are too broad. Hinn and Wood are not diminishing the influence of the Pentecostalism around the world. Indeed, there are places that if Pentecostal assemblies were not present, there would be no gospel of any kind present. What the authors strive to do is identify the bad apples in the barrel, those who have taken a deliberate leap into theological error and practice. Those who have twisted beyond recognition the pure Word of God. Their task is not an enviable one, but the outcome has been worth the risk.

Dr. Woodrow Kroll
Former President and Senior Bible Teacher for Back to the Bible

When false teaching crept into the church, Jude laid aside his desire to write about the church's common salvation in order to expose and oppose false teachers. In *Defining Deception* Costi Hinn and Anthony Wood have done the same. Pulling no punches, Hinn and Wood have written a well-documented book that warns the church of the dangers of New Apostolic Reformation (NAR), a sprawling movement that is rife with false miracles and abuses of the Bible. For Christians unfamiliar with the origin, extent, and teaching of NAR, this book provides a theological history and a biblically-grounded refutation. It is a timely book that counters a pervasive form of false teaching today. May the Lord use *Defining Deception* to guard the true apostolic faith, rescue sheep ensnared by false teaching, and build up the church of Jesus Christ.

Dr. David Schrock

Adjunct Professor of Systematic Theology, Southern Baptist Theological Seminary, Louisville, Kentucky, and Pastor of Preaching and Theology, Occoquan Bible Church, Woodbridge, Virginia

"There is nothing new under the sun. Many times current untruths are nothing more than old repackaged heresies and Anthony Wood and Costi Hinn do a marvelous job of reaching into the spirit of our age and pulling us back to biblical boundaries. I'm thankful they've handled such a sensitive topic and helped us love God with all our heart, soul, mind and strength."

Mark Lee

Lead Pastor of VantagePoint Church, Eastvale, California

Words cannot express the enthusiasm I have for this book. Hundreds of millions of professing believers have been deceived by the soul-destroying heresies of the Word-Faith/New Apostolic Reformation movement. False teachers like Benny Hinn, Bill Johnson and others like them, past and present, have claimed false visions, uttered false prophecies, promoted fake miracles and have exploited the poor, the sick, the desperate and the widows for decades. Worst of all is that these wolves have distorted the very Gospel itself and sullied the name of Jesus Christ. I am profoundly grateful for this excellent resource given to us by Costi Hinn and Anthony Wood. *Defining Deception* will not only help you to understand the deadly dangers of this movement, it will also equip you to speak the truth in love (Eph. 4:15) to those trapped in it and, by God's grace, see them delivered by truth. I joyfully commend this work to you.

Justin Peters
Evangelist, Author of *Clouds Without Water*

There is no question that the church today is at a loss in explaining the existence and veracity of the modern charismatic movement. In *Defining Deception: Freeing the Church from the Mystical-miracle Movement*, Costi W. Hinn and Anthony G. Wood have helped us understand this movement from the inside. These are men who experience the errors from within and now are speaking out against it. Their explanation is thorough, lucid, and charitable. In their winsome way, they help the believer come to grips with the dangers of the movement and the importance of Biblical literacy in the life of the church. In addition, their application to a contemporary church makes the lessons in the book practical and applicable. I learned much from these authors and recommend it as a source both in comprehending the movement and in helping others avoid it and even come out of it.

Dr. Alex Montoya
Pastor of First Fundamental Bible Church, Whittier, California

In 2 Chronicles 5:14, when the glory of God filled the temple in a cloud, the priests could not stand and minister nor could they enter. They ra-ther fell on their faces in reference. Yet Bethel Church in Redding, CA, regularly boasts that God visits them in glory clouds: gold glitter that falls from the ceiling during their worship services which they dance in and take pictures of. Worse than fooling people with their charismatic fakery is Bethel's false teaching, leading many astray from the sound words of our Lord Christ. Costi Hinn and Anthony Wood have done a judicious job with this book, not just alerting readers to the latest stream of char-ismaticism but educating about its earliest influences. They are pastoral and needfully direct, all in keeping with the command to hold firm to the trustworthy word as taught, and rebuke those who contradict it (Ti-tus 1:9).

Gabriel Hughes
Voice and creator, When We Understand the Text (WWUTT)

When I was first in ministry a wise older pastor told me "You are called to be a shepherd. That means you need to feed the sheep and sometimes chase the wolves. However, if you spend all your time chasing wolves the sheep with starve to death." While I prefer to read about being better at feeding the sheep, sometimes we need a book like *Defining Deception* to help us chase the wolves. Wood and Hinn have written a clear, concise warning about the rise of Third Wave/New Apostolic Reformation teachers. Clearly, they are wolves that need to be chased out of Christianity before they devour more of the sheep.

Dr. Paul Allen Smith
Pastor of First Baptist of Chandler, Arizona, and Professor of Old Testament, Gateway Seminary, Ontario, California

In the spirit of Titus 1:9, Costi Hinn and Anthony Wood have given the church a powerful book that is both instructive and corrective. *Defining Deception* is a robust examination of one of the deadliest spiritual heresies of our day. This is discernment at its finest; loving yet overtly truthful. I pray that scores of experience-addicted churchgoers will run from such mystical error and embrace the true, biblical gospel of Jesus Christ!

Nate Pickowicz
Pastor of Harvest Bible Church, Gilmanton Iron Works, New Hampshire, and author of *Why We're Protestant*

The careful research presented in this bold book is extremely helpful in assessing the validity of the mystical-miracle movement with its false claims and scandalous manipulation. Written with the insights gained as insiders, this book is Biblically accurate, historically based and compellingly written. It is a must read for any believer who seeks to "contend for the faith that was once for all delivered to the saints."

Dr. Les Lofquist
Executive Director of IFCA International

These are strange times that we live in. The Church in large measure has adopted the spirit of the times of the Judges, where every man does that which is right in his own eyes (Judges 17:6; 21:25). Tony and Costi have done a service to the Church in adding their clarion call of warning regarding the deception that continues to grow within her walls. Tracing the history of unbiblical practices back to their roots and bringing the story forward to the poisonous fruit that is being promoted in ministries like Bill Johnson's Bethel Church and Jesus Culture music, these dear brothers speak not as outsiders, but those who have seen first-hand the deception that is inherent in these false ministries. Written with bold truth, yet with love for those caught up in these satanic schemes, *Defining Deception* seeks to set captives free by pointing those imprisoned in these lies to the liberating power of the true gospel of Jesus Christ.

Dr. Richard Bargas
Pastor-Teacher at Grace Baptist Church, Wilmington, California

DEFINING DECEPTION

FREEING THE CHURCH FROM
THE MYSTICAL-MIRACLE MOVEMENT

COSTI W. HINN
ANTHONY G. WOOD

Southern California Seminary Press
El Cajon, CA

DEFINING DECEPTION: Freeing the Church from the Mystical-Miracle
Movement

©2018 Costi W. Hinn And Anthony G. Wood
Fourth printing with corrections, May 2018.

Published by Southern California Seminary Press
El Cajon, CA

ISBN-13: 978-0-9864442-4-1
ISBN-10: 0-9864442-4-3

Cover artwork by Jonathan Pasquariello.

Unless otherwise noted, all Scripture quotations are from The New American
Standard Bible (NASB), copyright © by the Lockman Foundation, 1977.

Scripture quotations indicated (Phillips) are from The New Testament in Modern
English by J. B. Phillips, copyright © by J. B. Phillips 1960, 1972. Administered by
The Archbishops' Council of the Church of England.

CONTENTS

ACKNOWLEDGMENTS

A book of this complexity can only be written with strong support from a community of believers. Based on this, we are intensely grateful to all who provided their knowledge, wisdom, and talents to help this project succeed.

We're immensely grateful to our wives, Christyne and Breanne, who patiently allowed the many "days off" behind computer screens and in seminary libraries. Likewise, we're grateful to the older children, Ethan and Peyton, who did their best to keep the backyard quiet for dad [Anthony].

The pastors, elders, and members of Mission Bible Church have faithfully supported us through thick and thin, giving joyfully and sacrificially, so we could commit our entire life to serving Christ and His bride. Deserving special mention for this project are unsung editing heroes Jerad Beltz Esq., Jake Elliott, Freizel Mcintosh, Desmond Outlaw, and Jim Palmer.

We consider the team at Southern California Seminary true comrades in the quest for truth. Dr. J. R. Miller, Professor Cory M. Marsh, Dean James I. Fazio, and Jennifer Ewing, have gently but sternly guided our layman's writ toward a stalwart theological form.

A personal debt is owed to Dr. Les Lofquist, Dr. Richard Bargas, and members of IFCA International who've supported vital elements of our local church development. Likewise, Dr. John MacArthur, Phil Johnson, Jay Flowers, and the team at Grace to You have spiritually blessed us beyond words over the past few years. The close friendship of men like Justin Peters, and professors from both Midwestern Baptist Theological Seminary [Costi], and Gateway Seminary of the SBC [Anthony] have also been a consistent vein of encouragement and counsel. Also, to the thousands of pastors who have been fighting the good fight on the issues brought forth in this book long before we wrote, thank you for your faithfulness–we're standing with you.

Finally, we thank the Lord, for providing us with His perfect Word unto faith and practice. May our children, and children's children, cherish it as we do.

FOREWORD

Since the 1990s the charismatic movement has seen explosive growth and unprecedented acceptance among mainstream evangelicals. Several factors have propelled this growth, starting with the lack of genuine spiritual life (meaning the absence of the Holy Spirit's power) among a generation of churchgoers benumbed by seeker-friendly methodologies and malnourished by being deprived of biblical teaching. One other significant catalyst in the growth of charismatic influence is the fact that honest, thorough, biblically informed, and up-to-date examinations of charismatic claims are almost impossible to come by. It is as if the broad evangelical community quietly mandated a moratorium on any criticism of the charismatic movement about the time the "holy laughter" craze began to ebb in the mid-1990s.

Defining Deception by Costi Hinn and Anthony Wood goes a long way toward filling that gap. This is a rich and provocative insiders' look at current charismatic trends, focusing on Bethel Church in Redding, CA—currently the Mecca for wannabe prophets and phony miracle workers. Bethel Redding is a hotbed of counterfeit wonders, false prophecies, and aberrant teachings. There may be an otherworldly spirit behind all the noise and confusion there, but it is certainly not the Holy Spirit.

To their credit, Hinn and Wood make an evenhanded examination of the strange phenomena and distinctive doctrines currently emanating from Bethel and coursing through the charismatic community. This is a well-written, well-documented, honest, careful, courageous, and biblically sound look at a worldwide movement that threatens to reshape and redefine Christianity. What Hinn and Wood have given us is an invaluable resource that could well prove to be one of the most important books of the decade.

Dr. John F. MacArthur
Pastor-Teacher of Grace Community Church, Sun Valley, California,
President of The Master's University and Seminary, and
President of Grace to You

EDITOR'S NOTE

I am pleased, as the editor for Defining Deception, to introduce you to the authors and some of the details of their life which have shaped them for writing this book. As a kid along for the ride in his childhood years, then as an adult employee, Costi has traveled the world with his Uncle Benny Hinn and seen first-hand the exploitation of thousands with the false gospel of healing and prosperity. Later, Costi was transformed by the power of the true Gospel of Jesus Christ and saw the theological errors he'd been adhering to. After his conversion, Costi was encouraged to pursue a Master of Divinity degree that enabled him to grow in his faith. At that time of spiritual maturation, Costi found a deep love for Christian history along with the orthodox teachings that have kept the church on course for two-thousand years. Recognizing his own sordid past in promoting the mystery-miracle movement, Costi reached out to family members and begged them to stop preaching the prosperity gospel and guaranteeing health and wealth in this life. He pleaded with many to turn to the Scriptures on all matters. He also reached out to close family members who partnered with movements like Bethel, Jesus Culture, and the New Apostolic Reformation preachers like Bill Johnson and Todd White. Costi cared about the truth and the spiritual well-being of his family and wanted to see them freed from those oppressive bonds.

Anthony has dedicated many years to his theological training and is pursuing his doctorate at Gateway Seminary. To match his education, Anthony has ministered with young adults in America and Asia since 2002. He founded a weekly ministry that reached more than 2,000 college students in 2007, he continues to speak at national conferences, and joined with Costi in the early years of a church plant in 2012. They've served together at Mission Bible Church of Tustin, CA ever since.

Anthony's awareness of the modern mystical-miracle movement began during his time serving college students who regularly approached him with a message they "heard from the Lord." In early 2012 a youth musician attempted to counsel Anthony on Bill Johnson's doctrine of

apostolic succession, suggesting that their church "needed an apostle."
But it wasn't until 2014 that Anthony began writing extensively against
Bethel's errors, and this only after a valued church member described
immense confusion due to Bethel's media podcasts and music. At this
point it became clear to Anthony that false teachers were, in fact, using
global media to target the core of local churches. After working with
thousands of young adults bridging two continents, Anthony knows
firsthand the destruction that results from those who rely upon subjective experience as the barometer of truth. In accordance with Titus
1:11, he believes that these false teachers must be held to account.

The heart of both Costi and Anthony is to help those caught in
deception discover that they are not alone. There is a real power in salvation and a real hope in Jesus Christ that far outweighs the temporal
prosperity they have been promised. It is my own prayer that everyone
who reads this book will come away with a new-found hope in the Gospel of Jesus Christ that does not impute shame, but instead frees us
from the shackles of these mystical-miracle movements.

God bless in your journey,

J.R. Miller
Professor of Applied Theology and Leadership
at Southern California Seminary

PREFACE:
HEART OF THE AUTHORS

Any man who dares to raise the charge of unintentional or intentional heresy against another must do so with humility and biblical evidence, ultimately requesting others within the true circle of Christian belief to carefully consider the assessment. And this is why we've written this book, requesting that every Christian examine the teaching and conduct of the "Third Wave/New Apostolic Reformation (NAR)"[1] movement. To allow readers their best look at these teachings, we'll shed light on the most famous leaders in the movement. Specifically, Bethel Church in Redding, California, and its senior pastor Bill Johnson, will serve to represent NAR. Bethel Church founded the globally recognized and mainstream worship brands (and bands) of Bethel Music and Jesus Culture. Our goal is to give readers the information needed to discern whether Bethel's teaching falls within the bounds of Christian orthodoxy or harms the advance of the gospel of Jesus Christ.

An effort of this nature demands prefatory remarks to help further clarify the goal of the book and protect against undue animosity from some Christians that may, at first glance, be surprised, or offended, by our grit and honesty. We offer these principles in the order they're most often asked.

First, this book is *not intended as a refutation against those who consider themselves Pentecostal* or contend that revelatory gifts are active

---

[1] The Third Wave is a name associated with the 1980's effort of C. Peter Wagner at Fuller Seminary, with adherents such as John Wimber, to revive the signs of Pentecost. The first wave is connected with 20th century Pentecostalism, the second wave with the 1960's charismatic movement, and the third wave is the New Apostolic Reformation (NAR) which demands normative use of "signs and wonders." Some adherents now call the NAR a "fourth wave" but that is a discussion for another book.

in the church today.[2] We understand that many Pentecostals hold to historically orthodox doctrinal positions making them part of the Christian family. Important to this point is that Bill Johnson withdrew his membership from the Assemblies of God (the world's largest Pentecostal denomination) and the Assemblies of God have since outlined their opposition to the kind of positions that Johnson has long-held, namely, Dominionism and Kingdom Now Theology.[3] So let it be clear: although the misuse of revelatory gifts is related to the problems mentioned in this work, they are not the primary issue we hope to address. The primary issue at hand is Johnson's mishandling of historically accepted orthodoxy—something all should agree is problematic.

Second, *a quest for Scriptural clarity does not need to be hostile.* In our modern age many steer away from complex issues in an absurd attempt to avoid conflict. However, we submit that theological error can be addressed in a way that provides clarity without hostility. As Church historian Bruce Shelley wrote, "Church history shows us that Christian theology is not primarily a philosophical system invented by men in the quiet of an academic study. Doctrines were hammered out by men who were on the work crew of the church. Every plank in the platform of orthodoxy was laid because some heresy had arisen that threatened to change the nature of Christianity."[4] Although we do personally know

---

[2] Revelatory gifts is the name widely attributed to what Scripture names word of knowledge, word of wisdom, prophecy, and the discerning of spirits.

[3] For example, the official AG position statement reads: "Kingdom Now or Dominion theology. The thought that God's kingdom can come on earth with a little help from humankind is intriguing to those who advocate this approach to impacting society. Rather than scoffing at the promise of Christ's imminent return (2 Peter 3:3,4), this errant theology says that Jesus will not return until the Church takes dominion of the earth back from Satan and his followers. By taking control, through whatever means possible, of political, ecclesiastical, educational, economic, and other structures, Christians supposedly can make the world a worthy place for Christ to return and rule over. This unscriptural triumphalism generates other related variant teachings." General Presbytery of the Assemblies of God, "Endtime Revival—Spirit-led and Spirit-controlled: A Response Paper to Resolution 16," Assemblies of God, August 11, 2000, accessed January 9, 2018, https://ag.org/Beliefs/Topics-Index/Revival-Endtime-Revival-Spirit-Led-and-Spirit-Controlled.

[4] Bruce L. Shelley, *Church History in Plain Language* (Nashville, TN: Thomas

some of the people we've written about in this book, and therefore possess the knowledge of scandal and big business, we've attempted to refrain from name-calling or telling unsubstantiated stories, preferring to magnify the biblical and ministerial deficiencies instead. This is partly the reason for the supporting footnotes, allowing them be utilized as a tool for the learner rather than a club for the fanatic.

Third, *defending truth is a clear biblical mandate.* The Apostle Paul wrote to Timothy, "instruct certain men not to teach strange doctrines, nor to pay attention to myths and endless genealogies, which give rise to mere speculation rather than furthering the administration of God which is by faith" (1 Tim 1:3-4). Martin Luther likewise said, "An upright shepherd and minister must improve his flock by edification, and also resist and defend it; otherwise, if resisting be absent, the wolf devours the sheep."[5] The birth of the Church was surrounded by doctrinal debate. The early apologists, the Reformation, the Great Awakening, even the famed hymn "Amazing Grace" were all birthed in the midst of doctrinal debate. Thank God strong men and women have chosen truth over tolerance throughout history. In order to defend biblical truth from error, without muddying orthodox waters, this book is intended as a refutation of modern Third Wave style charismata, specifically the version practiced by Bill Johnson and apostles of the New Apostolic Reformation (NAR). We will not delve into differences between evangelicals, post-conservatives, or even academic liberals. In fact, we are asking *all* Christians—no matter their creed or conduct—to analyze the significant concerns related to the mystical-miracle movement and Johnson's version of faith and to unite against it. For those who ask, "What concern is it of yours?" we submit that when any teaching infiltrates the borders of our local churches, a pastor must be both soldier and shepherd. Furthermore, Christ Himself warns us against blaspheming the Holy Spirit so we, as ministers of truth, must confront any derogation of the Spirit's Person and work.

Nelson, 1982), 48.

[5] Martin Luther, *The Table Talk of Martin Luther*, trans. by William Hazlitt, (London: H. G. Bohn, 1857), 183.

Last, in the spirit of Matthew 5 *we did attempt to speak with leaders of Bethel Church but were refused.* We even asked family members partnered with Bill Johnson to allow us a private audience with him to discuss these matters privately and ask questions. This request was also refused. So, for the sake of those who question our attempt at "brother to brother" reconciliation, please know that our desire is to see the people of Bethel saved and appropriately living out their Christian faith according to what the Bible teaches.

Ultimately, this book is not about Bill Johnson; it is about all those who embrace the reformation tradition of *sola Scriptura* and whether the Bible stands as our deciding rule of faith and practice. Noted theologian William Hordern once said, "It often seems that the modern (church person) is trying to say, 'The Bible is inerrant, but of course this does not mean it is without errors!'"[6] Hordern's tongue-in-cheek assessment about the "elasticity of words" in the modern age perfectly describes the root evil of Bill Johnson and Bethel Church. As you will see, virtually nothing flowing from Bethel is grounded in a proper interpretation of Scripture. The Bethel movement is defined by their elastic interpretation of words used in the Bible, and it is for this reason Christians must *unite* in declaring this aberrant theology unacceptable to the body of Christ.

We surmise you will find this book unique, as it has been unique to write. There are portions that deal with theology proper and remain slightly technical while other portions are apologetic and read with much more ease. We tried to structure the book in a way that provides an outside-in perspective for the everyday reader or layman, beginning with the problems associated with the Third Wave, then describing the ancestry of the Third Wave movement, and finally detailing Bill Johnson's faulty theology and ministry practices as a dramatic influencer of the Third Wave, Fourth Wave, and the NAR movement.

---

[6] William Hordern, *New Directions in Theology Today*, vol. 1, *Introduction* (Philadelphia, PA: Westminster, 1966), 83, quoted in Millard Erickson, Paul Kjoss Helseth, and Justin Taylor, eds., *Reclaiming the Center: Confronting Evangelical Accommodation in Postmodern Times* (Wheaton, IL: Crossway, 2004), 324.

In some circles, the tide has begun to shift as sincere Christians worldwide have become aware of the confusion surrounding Bethel Church and Bill Johnson. For a peek into the lives of those harmed by these divisive movements, you can read some of their stories in Appendix 1. Based on this assessment we submit that the current Third Wave /NAR controversy will one day be viewed as a Godsend—used by the Holy Spirit to recapture those now lost in a corrupt theology and reignite a generation around the *authority* and *sufficiency* of God's Word.

In service of our Lord,

Costi W. Hinn
Anthony G. Wood

1

Gold Dust and Glory Clouds

Introduction

The young man approached me with a confident step. He was the drummer on our worship team. The service was about to begin. People were funneling through the church doors and from his look I could tell he wanted to tell me something urgent. I saw genuine passion in his eyes, and as he began to speak I sensed a quiver in his tone . . . *this must be really important* I thought . . . then he whispered . . .

"Anthony, I could be the apostle of our church!"

Honestly, when he said those words, a thousand thoughts coursed through my mind. An apostle? Did the apostle Paul play drums? Are there apostles for our age? Do apostles wear skinny jeans? Most importantly, "Who told this young man *he* was an apostle?" This conversation was my introduction to Bill Johnson, Bethel Church, and Jesus Culture—the movement of young adults from Redding, California, that consider themselves equal with first century apostles, wielding supposed signs and wonders as evidence.

Christian empathy requires, at some level, we identify with the young man who approached me that Sunday morning. He was no wolf, no charlatan, and no false teacher. He was a passionate seeker. Sincere, but sincerely misguided. Millions of churchgoers find themselves in the same boat—hearing things online, entering a church, and thinking something akin to . . .

> I long for a deep connection with God that's meaningful and passionate. Do I have to wear a suit and sing hymns to be a biblical Christian? Do I have to do church the same way my parents did? Can I not shout with excitement because Christ set me free from sin and death without the gawking stares of elders? Can we keep having potlucks while the world starves? Is there no merit to my

feelings simply because some have taken emotionalism too far? I want to experience life in Christ to the fullest! Express myself. Fight for justice. Love truth. Change the world.

Sometimes I feel like my pastor is just trying to pacify my enthusiasm while he hates on the way "other churches" do things. But my mother always encouraged me to follow my heart and love everyone. My professors taught me to express myself freely and think outside the box. My generation is the most tolerant in history . . . shouldn't Christians be just as tolerant? Isn't there enough hatred in the world today already? We can do better!

I've heard of that place in Redding, California, that offers answers and experience. It's a place where children heal the sick, the arts are celebrated, and anyone can be just like Jesus. I think I've had enough of the stuffy old 'God in a box religion.' I can testify that pretty suits, fake smiles, and hymns didn't keep my parents from divorcing.

Maybe it is true . . . there's a better way? I felt ultra-loved at that conference. They've been inviting me to join their school and be a part of changing the world ever since . . . maybe it's time I take a step of real faith. No more God in a box for me. . . .

There's no doubt this line of reasoning is compelling for a group of lost and hurting young people. Anthropologists declare America is now a post-truth culture with 80 million millennials desperate to find answers.[1] Few in this generation believe in the shallow results of the entertainment-driven church, and even fewer are satisfied with the "stuffy" methods of churches they feel have hindered the joy of worship with rigid traditions. Unfortunately, in rejecting the methods of worship, many of these young people also rejected the foundational doctrines of the Christian faith. For so many, the search for the next emotional experience replaced the passion to search the Scripture for direction and guidance from God.[2] A growing number of these young

---

[1] Andrew Calcutt, "The Truth About Post-Truth Politics," *Newsweek*, November 21, 2016, accessed January 2, 2018, http://www.newsweek.com/truth-post-truth-politics-donald-trump-liberals-tony-blair-523198.
[2] David J. McClead, "Counterfeit Revival," *Emmaus Journal* 7, no.1 (1996): 73.

adults are now married with children and beginning to realize the stress and confusion that comes when you base the Christian life on subjective religious experiences. A few questions they ask: What is my role in marriage if not defined by Scripture? How do we raise our children if not defined by Scripture? What if my spouse senses a new "word from God" and I don't agree?

One of our readers from Europe recently emailed explaining her "exasperation" from trying to hold a marriage together with a husband immersed in the mystical-miracle movement. She described her disagreements with him about raising their two children, explaining she would turn to Scripture for answers, while he refuted her findings with his own experience of a personal "word from the Lord." For her, her husband's subjective opinions, with God's name attached, have pushed her to the limit. Ungrounded experiences like this, and others, can lead couples to divorce because there is no common foundation on which they can come together, test the claims, and make decisions. In the seminal book *Forged From Reformation*, published by Southern California Seminary, Thomas Ice describes how the 20th century retreat from sound Bible teaching led our nation to repeat the errors of the past and embrace a religion based on mystical experience:

> Historians have noticed that culture cycles back-and-forth between rationalism and mysticism over the years. Since the 1960's, American culture has definitely moved in the direction of and is now firmly dominated by a mystical worldview. Biblical Christianity is not based on reason or mysticism as its starting point for truth; instead, it is built upon revelation of God's word. When mysticism dominates a culture's mindset then it predisposes one hermeneutically toward mysticism and non-literal interpretation. . . . This was the situation in the late Middle Ages when the Reformation was sparked by the Holy Spirit and has produced the last 500 years of a more biblical culture within Protestantism and a much more biblically vibrant Christianity. That era appears to be coming to an end in the United States as the church clearly is sinking into an overall swamp of mysticism, shifting away from a bibliocentric focus.[3]

---

[3] Thomas Ice, "Dispensationalism and the Reformation," in *Forged From Reformation: How Dispensational Thought Advances the Reformed Legacy*, ed. by

So much has changed since that morning years ago when I was confronted by the drummer-apostle. Bethel Church, and their band Jesus Culture, has grown in influence and the theology of apostolic succession has crisscrossed the globe—influencing young adults of every nation.[4] Along with the music, there's been an abundance of bizarre ministry practices which have hit the headlines. Here are a few examples from Bethel Church, which will be detailed later:

- Bethel youth travel to rest on graves of historic leaders "sucking" their spirit.
- Beni Johnson, wife of Bill Johnson, teaches that she speaks personally with angels.
- Bethel youth walk through fire tunnels and frolic in groups on the floor.
- Feathers and gold dust are said to miraculously fall from the ceiling during Bethel worship.
- Bethel parishioners are told to breathe on others to make them whole.
- Many congregants at Bethel shake and roll like the eastern mystics of Kundalini.
- Bill Johnson teaches that God wants *everyone* healthy, and sickness is evidence of sin.

These outrageous stories are all part of a larger confluence historically called the Third Wave or word-of-faith movement, and now modernly termed the NAR. These movements include myriads of young adults led by a group of spiritual fathers and mothers who "name and claim" the earth through tongues, dreams, and miracles. In essence, they believe there is a "law of faith" which exists in the universe and the more one believes, the more likely something is going to happen.

Admittedly, we [the authors] know this movement well. We've seen the backstage planning of a "miracle" crusade, the pre-selection of those to be healed, the bravado in the green rooms, the falsified twitter

Christopher Cone and James I. Fazio (El Cajon, CA: Southern California Seminary Press, 2017), 29, 30.

4 Bob Smietana,"The 'Prophets' and 'Apostles' Leading the Quiet Revolution in American Religion," *Christianity Today*, August 3, 2017, accessed August 3, 2017, http://www.christianitytoday.com/ct/2017/august-web-only/bethel-church-international-house-prayer-prophets-apostles.html.

feeds, the manipulation of youthful naïveté, and even the post event cash-money exchanges behind hotel doors in some destitute third world nation . . . nothing but smoke and mirrors.

Miracle Manipulation

The question arises, Is this kind of miracle-manipulation part of church history? Is there any insight from the Bible that warns Christians about false-teachers and false-miracles? Acts 8 indicates that we are not the first to face this problem:

> When Simon saw how the Spirit was given through the apostles' laying their hands upon people he offered them money with the words, "Give me this power too, so that if I were to put my hands on anyone he could receive the Holy Spirit." But Peter said to him, "To hell with you and your money! How dare you think you could buy the gift of God! You can have no share or place in this ministry, for your heart is not honest before God. All you can do now is to repent of this wickedness of yours and pray earnestly to God that the evil intention of your heart may be forgiven. For I can see inside you, and I see a man bitter with jealousy and bound with his own sin!" (Acts 8:18–23, Phillips).

Not only is miracle manipulation part of the biblical record, it has been a challenge to the genuine work of God throughout history. Dating back to A.D. 156 one can research the assault on orthodox Christianity by perhaps the first charlatan of the church, Montanus. Montanus came from Asia Minor along with two "prophetesses" named Prisca and Maximilla. His sect of followers insisted that opposition to their versions of prophecy was blasphemy against the Holy Spirit and their deception caused many churches to split.[5] Sound familiar?

The medieval Roman Catholic Church was infiltrated by similar tricksters famous for evoking supposed miracles to enhance their authority. Some tried to prove their false doctrine of purgatory by claiming to bring people back from the dead. Sir Keith Thomas, a noted historian at Oxford writes, "The medieval Church thus found

---

[5] Cf. Shelley, *Church History in Plain Language*, 65.

itself saddled with the tradition that the working of miracles was the most efficacious means of demonstrating its monopoly of truth."[6]

The Renaissance humanist and Roman Catholic priest Erasmus spoke strongly against the forms of "ecclesiastical trickery" prevalent in his day. In his collection of dialogues titled *The Repentant Girl*, Erasmus describes the nuns of a convent frightening new members with the appearance of a ghost, calling in the priest to exorcise a ghost who wasn't there! He writes, "These are the ones of whom I speak, the ones who find joy in either hearing or telling monstrous lies and strange wonders. They never get enough of such stories, so long as prodigies are recounted, involving banshees, goblins, devils or the like."[7]

In more recent history, global accounts of signs, wonders, and tongues-speaking, have been associated with a change of brain state and psychological trauma. Studies have been done which Keener concludes link these trance like states and glossolalia to the same kind of demonic possession present in the Kalabari spirits of Zulu religion.[8]

Defining "Miracle"

Because the falsifying of miracles didn't begin with Bethel Church or Bill Johnson, and in fact runs through the course of church history, it is important that we begin our assessment by defining what is considered a true miracle vs. what is considered a false miracle. Is a cloud of glitter dust really God's work? Are falling feathers a sign of angels? Can a seemingly revelatory dream come from God, a demon, or the imagination? Knowing the biblical definition of a miracle will provide us a litmus as we study the many egregious acts of historic charlatans and frauds.

---

[6] Keith Thomas, *Religion and the Decline of Magic* (London, UK: Oxford University Press, 1971), 26. Many scholars believe this is why John Calvin adopted a quasi-non-miracle stance.

[7] Desiderius Erasmus, *The Praise of Folly*, ed. and trans. Hoyt H. Hudson (Prin-ceton, NJ: Princeton University Press, 1970), 55.

[8] For more on controversial instances of tongues related to witchcraft and mediums see: Craig S. Keener, *Acts: An Exegetical Commentary* (Grand Rapids, MI: Baker Academic, 2012), 1:817; cf. Craig S. Keener, "Spirit Possession as a Cross-Cultural Experience," *Bulletin for Biblical Research* 20, no. 2 (2010): 215-235. See also, James Douglas, "The Divine Immanency," *Bibliotheca Sacra* 45, no. 180 (1888): 567-584.

For the sake of brevity and fairness, let's use a definition of miracles that could be accepted by a wide range of scholars and churchmen. Biblically speaking, a miracle is an observable phenomenon delivered powerfully (*dynamis*) by God directly or indirectly through an authorized agent whose extraordinary character captures the immediate attention (*teras*) of the viewer, points to something beyond the phenomenon (*sēmeion*), and is a distinctive work (*ergon*)—whose source can be attributed to no one else but God.[9] Regarding miracles, the Bible uses the word "sign" (Hebrew, *oth*; Greek, *sēmeion*), the word "wonder" (Hebrew, *mopeth*; Greek, *teras*), and "mighty work" (Hebrew, *gburah*; Greek, *dynamis*). Most have heard these terms conjoined as "signs and wonders" always used in the context of inspiring awe and amazement that (God) or some(one) extraordinary is at work.[10] A simple way of saying it would be: *a miracle is God suspending, or working counter to, natural laws and personally reaching into life to rearrange people and their circumstances according to his will.*[11]

The basis of this definition is that whether we consider a floating axe head (2 Kings 6:6) or water turned to wine (John 2:1-11), or a man crippled forty years suddenly jumping up and down (Acts 3:8), the events were clearly outside the observable laws of nature. Note, this definition does not assert miracles themselves have ceased (a common misapprehension by opponents of classic cessationism)[12] but only that

---

[9] Wilhelm Mundle and Otfried Hofius, "Miracle, Wonder, Sign," in *The New International Dictionary of New Testament Theology*, ed. by Colin Brown (Grand Rapids, MI: Zondervan 1986) 2:620-35. An extensive article on New Testament vocabulary for miracles can be found here.

[10] Ibid., 226. See also, John MacArthur and Richard Mayhue, eds. *Biblical Doctrine: A Systematic Summary of Bible Truth* (Wheaton, IL: Crossway, 2017), 216; and, Wayne Grudem, *Systematic Theology: An Introduction to Biblical Doctrine* (Grand Rapids, MI: Zondervan, 1994), 356.

[11] This is an aggregate definition coalesced from modern evangelical theologians such as, Millard Erickson, *Christian Theology* (Grand Rapids, MI: Baker Books, 1998), 431-434; Wayne Grudem, *Systematic Theology*, 355-375; and, John MacArthur and Richard Mayhue, *Biblical Doctrine*, 217.

[12] We take cessationism to mean the theology that the sign-gifts given by the Holy Spirit evidenced in the book of Acts ceased to operate in the church with the death of the twelve apostles. This in no way means that God ceases to do miracles in the church today, but that these are not normative or given as signs to confirm the Gospel of Jesus Christ. For further investigation of this topic see,

what *qualifies* as a biblical miracle is much more robust than often offered by Third Wave/NAR and many charismatic proponents. Clearly, this is not an attack on the supernatural but actually is intended to strengthen respect for the supernatural because if we define everything as a miracle we lose the ability to recognize when a real miracle takes place.

Many modern faith healers cite Jon Mark Ruthven's book, *On the Cessation of the Charismata*, as exegetical evidence for their ministry activities. Ruthven's work attempts to build a biblical case for signs and wonders, stating, "miracles manifest the essential core activity of [Christ's] mission; to displace the physical and spiritual ruin of the demonic kingdom by the wholeness of the Kingdom of God."[13] In the book, Ruthven's primary agenda is to refute B. B. Warfield's formative work *Counterfeit Miracles*.[14] Sadly, Ruthven's base premise is mired in inference and unsound exegesis, confusing Scripture, merging and distorting distinct promises for national Israel with the modern church, misrepresenting classical cessationism, and using hermeneutical ploys to offer an unsupported study of the New Testament word "power."[15] Ruthven acknowledges his views remain well outside those of respected "open but cautious" theologians such as Wayne Grudem and D. A. Carson. He himself admits, "New Testament scholars may cringe at (my) easy leap between the Ephesian and Matthean traditions."[16] Thus,

---

Mark A. Snoeberger, "Tongues—Are They for Today?," *Detroit Baptist Seminary Journal* 14 (2009): 3-21. See also Philip A. Craig, "'And Prophecy Shall Cease': Jonathan Edwards on the Cessation of the Gift of Prophecy," *Westminster Theological Journal* 64, no. 1 (2002): 163-184.

[13] Jon Mark Ruthven, *On the Cessation of the Charismata* (Tulsa, OK: Word & Spirit Press, 2011), 101.

[14] Benjamin B. Warfield, *Counterfeit Miracles* (New York, NY: Charles Scribner's Sons, 1918).

[15] Central to Ruthven's misanalysis are: (1) consistent use of Old Testament promises given solely to Israel as evidence of church-age charismata (Ruthven, *On the Cessation of the Charismata*, xxii, 100, 185, 233); (2) propagating without exegetical evidence that power (*dynamis*) equates to revelatory charismata in Paul's epistles when context shows otherwise (Ibid., 140, 142, 145, 158, et al.); and (3) using inference to rebut historically held orthodox positions, often employing terms of mitigation or inference such as "may, apparent, or speculate" without Scriptural support (Ibid., 142, 143, 144, 145, 147, 149, 151 157, 159, 189, et al.).

[16] Ibid., 209.

by his own admittance, Ruthven's exegesis of the Bible falls outside the fences of theological reliability, and, consequently, we conclude his work provides a faulty foundation on which to build any belief or ministry.

Returning to our own definition of miracles, its strength lies in that it doesn't cross into deism (eliminating God's direct interaction with the world) and recognizes His ongoing providential guidance. Sovereignty demands God's eternal decree and continual providential work in, through, and unto His creation (Rom 11:36). This means that even when He's not conducting miracles, the power of God's word is providentially guiding all things to His perfectly determined end. In essence, God who works a miracle by stilling the sun in the sky, also works providentially by causing your tax refund to show up at just the right moment!

Based on this accepted definition of miracles, we must immediately admit that many, if not most, of the miracles done by modern healers or self-styled prophets are not really miracles at all. These men and women are not stopping the sun, walking on water, turning water into wine, or even instantly healing a lifelong ailment. Even if they are infusing some kind of healing, it is simply God's providential and precious timing based on prayer. Renowned Bible teacher John MacArthur once shared:

> The types of miracles that are being claimed today are absolutely nothing like New Testament miracles. In fact, the types of miracles today could be distinctly seen as different than New Testament miracles. Jesus and the apostles instantly and completely healed people born blind, a paralytic, a man with a withered arm. All obvious and indisputable miracles, even Jesus' enemies didn't challenge the reality of His miracles that He had the people there to verify them [sic]. He raised the dead, of course, as we well know. They never did a miracle that was slow, they never did a miracle that took time, and they never did a miracle that was less than permanent. By contrast, most modern miracles are partial, gradual, temporary, sometimes reversed, and impossible to verify.[17]

---

[17] John MacArthur, "Does God Do Miracles Today?" Grace To You, August 11, 1991, accessed August 03, 2017, https://www.gty.org/library/sermons-library/90-56/does-god-do-miracles-today.

We need to be careful when documenting supposed miracles. Even more vital to this book, however, is that the major defining characteristic of New Testament miracles was that they were used by God to *authenticate of the Gospel of Jesus Christ*. For instance, Nicodemus acknowledged that the signs Jesus worked were from God (John 3:2); God validated Jesus through "signs and wonders and various miracles" (Heb 2:4); the Samaritan woman testified about Jesus' supernatural knowledge about her life (John 4:29); Philip performed exorcisms, healings, and other signs as he proclaimed the Messiah (Acts 8:6–8); the residents of Lydda and Sharon affirmed God's work in healing Aeneas (Acts 9:35); the disciples also practiced this (Matt 10:7–8; 9:35; Acts 8:13). True New Testament miracles always pointed to the person of Christ. Therefore, if the glory of God and the Good News of Christ aren't clarified or enhanced by a supposedly extraordinary act, it isn't a miracle of God. Yet, if it's not of God, then who is it from? This will occupy much of what follows.[18]

Conclusion

In summary, true miracles are outside the observed laws of nature and authenticate the Gospel and align with clear Gospel teachings. Miracle-manipulation existed in the early church, has continued throughout church history, and certainly creeps into many pockets of modern "name-it-and-claim-it" theology. Knowing these truths forces us to examine the miracle claims of Bill Johnson and the Third Wave/NAR movement along with the tactics and theology used to promote these claims.

So, was our young drummer really an apostle? Are grave sucking and glory clouds really miracles? Is Beni Johnson, wife of Bill Johnson, really conversing with angels? And, is Bethel Church in Redding, California, really the nexus of God's next great work on planet Earth? Let's begin to answer those questions by looking at the past one hundred years, getting to know the men and women Bill Johnson reveres as generals of the faith.

---

[18] See Appendix 5 for a fuller discussion of this topic.

2

Hall of Generals

Introduction

Modern proponents of the Third Wave and New Apostolic Reformation claim a lineage of historic faith heroes as ancestral evidence that their actions represent God's will. Who are these supposed heroes? Are they truly men and women worthy of such praise? This chapter will examine the words and deeds of the people Bill Johnson has publicly lionized as generals of his faith.

Bethel Church's form of Third Wave/NAR theology has risen to an unprecedented level of global popularity. However, what many people don't realize is that the genesis of their movement began over 100 years ago in the United States with the rise of Pentecostalism. Since the early 20th century, the world has seen the number of people describing themselves as Pentecostal/Charismatic steadily increase from under a million in Africa during the early 1900's, to over 500 million worldwide by the year 2000 (See Table 2.1 below). It is not a coincidence that the rise of global charismata occurred during a time when self-acclaimed prophets and faith healers began selling to impoverished peoples an upgraded version of Christianity focused on quick healing and financial blessings from God. This new prosperity-gospel captivated audiences as they began to pack tents and stadiums. The demand has grown and the spiritual stock market has been ripe for a massive payday ever since. Today's faith-healers are raking in the biggest paychecks in church history.

Table 1. Global expansion of Pentecostals/Charismatics, 1900–2000 (in millions)

Continent	1900		2000	
	Adherents	%	Adherents	%
Africa	.9	.8	126.0	16.1
Asia	0	0	134.9	3.7
Europe	0	0	37.6	5.2
Latin America	0	0	141.4	27.2
North America	0	.1	79.6	25.7
Oceania	0	0	4.3	14

Sources: Adapted from Bruce Shelley, Church History in Plain Language, 4th ed. (Nashville, TN: Thomas Nelson, 2013), 498; Table 2.2 Evangelical and Pentecostal-Charismatic Adherents (in millions), Mark Noll, The New Shape of World Christianity: How American Experience Reflects Global Faith (Downers Grove, IL: Intervarsity Press, 2009), 22; and Table 1-4 Adherents of all Religions on 6 Continents, AD 1900-2000, David B. Barrett, George T. Kurian, and Todd M. Johnson, eds., World Christian Encyclopedia, 2nd ed. (New York: Oxford University Press, 2001), 1:13-15.
Note: Percentages of adherents within the total population of the continent.

In a significant way, this explosion of Third Wave/NAR prosperity-based church life is vastly different from the life Jesus described for his followers. Jesus taught that things would be difficult for those who stood for truth (Matt 10:22), and that even loving families would be divided (Luke 21:16–19). Jesus never prophesied his followers winning a global popularity contest or recipients of untold financial wealth. In stark contrast to these ideas, Jesus promised severe persecution for those who dared followed him (John 16:2). Is the globalization of Third Wave /NAR theology compatible with the description of the few who are finding the abundant life? Or, can it be said that this unimaginable popularity is the result of ear tickling and clever marketing? Let's do some digging to find out.

As we tour the last century of Pentecostal/Charismatic history, the research reveals that not everyone within these movements taught or accepted outright heresy. Furthermore, many of today's Pentecostals and Charismatics no longer claim allegiance to some of these extreme theologies. The men and women on this list of generals, however, did distort key Christian doctrines and contributed to the chaos we're seeing today in the Third Wave/NAR movements. The following biographies are not a direct or implied judgment on the salvation of these individuals or a broad brush indictment on the Pentecostal/Charismatic movement at large. Still, it is vitally important that we weigh these teachings and lifestyles in light of the New Testament standard concerning keeping teachers accountable (Eph 4:11-16; 2 Tim 2:15; Titus 2:7-8; James 3:1). From this standard we can determine if these individuals preached Christ, or contributed to the present chaos by their errors, or by preaching another gospel (Gal 1:6-12).

When analyzing the life and ministry of these people it's important to remember that every pastor has a past, and even the best men and women have flaws. There is an incredible amount of unconditional grace available to every Christian, including pastors! What pastor hasn't preached a bad sermon, misquoted a text, or recognized flaws in their theology as their biblical understanding grew? Yet, the qualifications for church leaders are clearly listed in 1 Timothy 3 and Titus 1. What stands out in these lists is that other than the ability to teach, they emphasize a leader's character.[1] Furthermore, the epistle of James does not provide amendments or loopholes for those teaching in the church—a teacher is held to a stricter standard in judgment: "Not many of you should become teachers, my brothers, for you know that we who teach will be judged with greater strictness" (James 3:1).

Even in the most balanced sense, the lives and ministries of people in this lineage of Third Wave/NAR history were littered with false teaching, false healings, and false hope. The result of their ministries have been the destruction of lives, constant controversy, unbiblical lifestyles, and a collective failure to remain faithful to the Gospel of

---

[1] J. R. Miller, *Elders Lead a Healthy Family: Shared Leadership for a Vibrant Church* (Eugene, OR: Wipf and Stock Publishers, 2017), 52-63. Here, Miller explains each character quality that biblical church leaders should possess to be effective as Christ's servants.

Jesus Christ. This is, unfortunately, the hard evidence splattered throughout Pentecostal/Charismatic history.

A seasoned pastor once advised, "preach with a moist eye." In that same heart, we want you to understand that these biographical sketches are painted through tears. The past century of Pentecostal/Charismatic history is absolutely heart-breaking. Millions have lived and died under the guile of false teachers and millions more continue on the path of destruction. Christians need accurate information so they can make informed decisions with regards to the misleading miracles and exercise discernment with any teacher who claims a heritage from these teachers. Furthermore, true believers need to be prayerful, faithful, and resilient in reaching out to those caught in this net of deceit. In many (if not, most) cases, salvation is on the line. Jude writes, "And have mercy on some, who are doubting; save others, snatching them out of the fire; and on some have mercy with fear, hating even the garment polluted by the flesh" (Jude 22–23).

Today, a new generation of leaders is seeking to emulate and preserve their legacy through ministries such as Bill Johnson's "House of Generals" project.[2] Based on all of this, let's examine the Third Wave /NAR family tree.

Charles F. Parham (1873–1929)

Charles F. Parham has been called both "The Father of Pentecost" and "The Father of Apostolic Faith." His unique ministry of Baptism of the Spirit, evidenced by speaking in tongues, began at his Topeka, Kansas, Bible School in 1901. Parham's new theology formed a bridge between the late 19th century holiness movements and the founding of Pentecostalism in the early 20th century.[3] Parham rejected all existing

---

[2] Originally, "House of Generals," Bill Johnson Ministries, accessed September 30, 2016, http://bjm.org/house-of-generals. The video has since been removed from the website, but reference to it can also be found at "Video: Bethel Church Leader Creates Library to Honor Past Revivalists," *Charisma Magazine*, accessed December 13, 2017, https://www.charismamag.com/site-archives/570-news/featured-news/13653-videobethel-church-leader-creates-library-to-honor-past-revivalists.

[3] Robert Owens, "The Asuza Street Revival: The Pentecostal Movement Begins in America," in *The Century of the Holy Spirit: 100 Years of Pentecostal and Charismatic Renewal, 1901–2001,* ed. Vinson Synan (Nashville, TN: Thomas Nelson, 2001), 42ff; Vinson Synan, interview by Craig von Buseck, "The Early Days of the

forms of religious authority and this rebellious attitude made him a compelling leader for many unsatisfied people. As a young Methodist pastor, he showed a lot of promise in the pulpit, but was in constant conflict with denominational leaders whom he believed to be narrow-minded about his ministry methods.[4]

Parham claimed to believe in the Bible, but rejected the notion that Christian orthodoxy should set any limits on his own interpretation. Like many ambitious teachers, he had a quite creative theological imagination and was equally controversial. In contradiction to his claim of following biblical teachings, he openly rejected the idea of an eternal hell; thinking it to be out of step with God's character. Denying that God's dignity existed in every human, Parham was and remained a racist who kept close ties with the KKK.[5] His theology concerning the Baptism in the Holy Spirit and the necessity of tongues for full salvation, along with his later theology concerning healing, was remarkably different from biblical teaching.[6] Parham was unapologetic in teaching that speaking in tongues was required evidence of true salvation. Throughout his life, he continually adapted his teaching to accommodate various experiences, yet none of these revisions moved him closer to orthodox teaching. Such crippling doctrinal error caused many people to become confused and insecure about their salvation if they didn't speak in tongues. Then, and now, it is likely that many people speak in ecstatic tongues simply out of fear of being judged unsaved.[7] I [Costi] remember being a casualty of Parham's theology on

---

Pentecostal Movement," CBN, accessed January 24, 2018, http://www1.cbn.com /early-days-pentecostal-movement.

[4] Sarah Parham, *The Life of Charles F. Parham* (Joplin, MO: Hunter Printing, 1930), 23.

[5] James R. Goff Jr., *Fields White Unto Harvest: Charles F. Parham and the Missionary Origins of Pentecostalism* (Fayetteville, AR: University of Arkansas Press, 1988), 131; and, Walter J. Hollenweger, *Pentecostalism: Origins and Developments Worldwide* (Peabody, MA: Hendrickson Publishers, 1997), 19.

[6] Miller, *Promise of the Father*, 62–71. For a discussion of the biblical doctrine of Baptism in the Holy Spirit see, J. R. Miller, *Have You Not Yet Received the Spirit?: Finding Unity through the Baptism in the Holy Spirit* (San Diego, CA: Emerging Life Resources, 2008).

[7] For Parham's complete teaching on tongues as evidence of salvation see: Charles Parham, "Baptism of the Holy Ghost," in *A Voice Crying In The Wilderness* (1902; repr., Baxter Springs, KS: Parham, 1944).

tongues as a young boy. People were often coached at the altar as they desperately tried to obtain the spiritual level of everyone else who spoke in tongues. "Just begin to move your lips!," the pastor coached. "Just say whatever is on the tip of your tongue—it will not make sense to you but it makes sense to God," he clarified. In our world, tongues was evidence of the Holy Spirit's residence, essential for spiritual warfare, and the only way to shake off the stigma of being a second-class citizen in the church.

Parham paired his so-called "gospel preaching" with grand stories about his own supernatural power and the crowds could not resist him. Parham gained credibility with the desperate and sick by claiming he had healed his own son of a fever. He banned medicine from his home and vowed to never again trust anything but the Word of God.[8]

Beyond his own personal theology about the supernatural, Parham possessed the prototypical elitist mindset. When talking about other "less powerful" preachers, he was sure to explain that no one was as "anointed" in the same way he was. Although, he was willing to teach a person how to gain his power if he or she paid a fee for it. As an aside, this is exactly what we see today with the schools for signs and wonders sponsored by mystical-miracle faith healers like Benny Hinn, Bill Johnson, and Todd White—it's pay-to-play if you want to access their power.

To help expand his ministry, Parham and his wife started the Bethel Healing Home in Topeka, Kansas, thereby increasing their living by giving false hope to the hurting people who flocked to them for help. This "home" contained special healing rooms that still exist today.[9] Parham believed everyone would be healed if they only had enough faith to receive it—a formula that ignores the biblical truth surrounding the sovereignty of God in healing (John 5:1-9). This concept of faith—as a force that can control God's power—is used and taught by many healing ministries today, and if it doesn't work, they can blame the sick, but never, of course, the healer for a failed healing. At his healing home, Parham offered special classes for ministers and trained people for ministry who took his theology of healing nationwide. Despite his self-claimed power to heal, Parham was unable

---

[8] Roberts Liardon, *God's Generals: Why They Succeeded and Why Some Failed* (New Kensington, PA: Whitaker House, 1996), 114.

[9] See, for example, "Healing Rooms," Tree of Life Church, Topeka, KS, accessed September 30, 2016, http://www.treeoflifeks.org/healing-rooms.

to heal himself when his heart failed at just 55 years of age. Written by his wife, Parham's biography contributes to the legend of this deceptive leader, painting him as a hero of the Christian faith. Other Pentecostal/Charismatic leaders have immortalized him with sentiments like: "And when he left earth, he did so because he willed it. Although some will not accept Parham's ministry because of his support for the Ku Klux Klan, most remember Parham for his sacrificial love and primarily for his faithfulness."[10] Thankfully, credible sources like *Fields White unto Harvest*, authored by James R. Goff Jr, and *Promise of the Father* by J. R. Miller provide people with a more realistic picture of the self-proclaimed faith healer.

Parham was at best a confused man, whose life was marked by pride and his own rejection of the authority of Scripture. Ultimately, his ministry spiraled into obscurity surrounded by allegations of sodomy in 1907, but not before influencing one of his most prominent students, William Seymour. It was Seymour who would go on to cement his own legacy within the Pentecostal movement and launch its most experience-based insurgence into orthodox Christianity.

William Seymour (1870–1922)

William Seymour was credited with starting the Azusa Street Revival. Not only was he heavily influenced by Parham's theology about Spirit Baptism, healing and tongues, he also shared the same rebellious streak. Against the counsel of his mentor, Seymour quit Parham's Bible college after a few classes because he felt like God was calling him to launch out on his own. With no real biblical training, and some severely flawed theology under his belt, Seymour arrived in Los Angeles in February 1906. Within his first two months, he racked up quite a resume. First, he was locked out of a church for preaching false claims about tongues. Undeterred, Seymour swayed a small group to split from that church and began his own prayer meetings with his friend and housemate, Edward Lee. After Seymour laid hands on Lee, Lee began to speak in unknown tongues. Seymour did not have the gift of tongues himself, but apparently was able to impart it to his friend by supernatural means. Perhaps feeling left out and insecure that his followers would doubt his own supernatural power, Seymour claimed

---

[10] Liardon, *God's Generals*, 133.

to have received his own special gift of tongues three days later. Between those three days on April 9–12, 1906, the Azusa Street Revival began.[11]

One of Seymour's most prolific teachings was a confusing mixture of truth and error. He taught that Christ's atoning work on the cross meant that every believer is saved (truth), sanctified (truth), guaranteed healing in this life (false), and guaranteed to speak in tongues (false).[12] Based on his theology, if you weren't experiencing all four, you weren't experiencing the fullness of salvation. Much like Parham, Seymour would later change his position on tongues in his ongoing effort to appease his critics.

Like many of the heavyweight heroes in Pentecostal history, Seymour created two classes of Christians. Miller explains, "as Pentecostalism progressed, the most prominent and cohesive thrust became the emphasis of two distinct and separate stages of Christian faith; two classes of Christians, those who have the real power of God and those who do not."[13] Another distinctive of Seymour's ministry was how he communicated his erroneous doctrines. Seymour was people-conscious and thoughtful in his approach to teaching. He never used complex terms and was primarily focused on helping common folks learn how to be baptized with the Holy Spirit, speak in tongues, and get healed.[14] With such a personable approach to his false teaching, who wouldn't have followed Seymour?

Like most deceptive ministries, Seymour's was riddled with controversy. On just the short list, there were charges of racism toward Hispanics, countless false claims of miracles, and demonic behavior. Ironically, even his mentor Parham accused him of being "from the Devil" because of the outlandish and demonic manifestations transpiring in Azusa.[15]

---

[11] Azusa Street Mission, "The History of Azusa Street," accessed January 24, 2018, http://312azusa.com/william-seymour/. See also the Azusa Street Timeline.

[12] "Pentecost Has Come: The Apostolic Faith Movement," *The Apostolic Faith* 1, no. 1 (September 1906): 2, accessed January 9, 2018, http://apostolicfaith .org/library/historical/azusa-originals/Azusa-Paper-Original-01.pdf.

[13] Miller, *Promise of the Father*, 76–77.

[14] "Pentecost Has Come," 2.

[15] Miller, *Promise of the Father*, 79, 83.

Regardless of the controversy, the Azusa Street Revival gained enough momentum to establish the Pentecostal movement for good. Infecting the church with bizarre and unbiblical behavior, the revival's teaching birthed more self-described apostles who emerged from every corner of the nation. News of the movement spread and during that same time, Europe became enamored by the same deluding influence.

Smith Wigglesworth (1859-1947)

Wigglesworth was one of the first to take faith healing to violent new heights. He is considered Pentecostal and Charismatic royalty these days, but that's mostly because people are ignorant of his aberrant and unbiblical ministry tactics. For nearly two decades of my own life [Costi], Wigglesworth was one of my heroes because he represented audacious faith without any regard for the confines of religiosity and tradition. He was a reckless rebel and, just like Peter, was willing to jump over the side of the boat to walk on water and follow Jesus. *That's the kind of risk-taking that God always blesses,* I often thought. That's who I wanted to be!

Born before both Parham and Seymour, Wigglesworth outlived them both. Due to his long life span, he was perfectly positioned to almost single handedly impact the UK in the same way Parham and Seymour impacted America.

Wigglesworth focused the core of his ministry on signs and wonders like healing, miracles, and tongues. He taught that believers should refuse medical treatment for any illness. If not the first, he was *one* of the first in history to conduct his faith healing using methods other than laying on of hands—though he still touched them. According to Wigglesworth, sickness was evidence of demonic activity, so he would physically attack the person as though they were the devil! Ignoring biblical teaching that spiritual warfare has nothing to do with flesh and blood (Eph 6:12), Wigglesworth would punch, slap, or hit people in the place where they were afflicted. Wigglesworth explained his reason for assaulting sick people:

> There are some times when you pray for the sick and you are apparently rough. But you are not dealing with a person, you are dealing with the satanic forces that are binding that person. Your heart is full of love and compassion to all, but you are moved to a holy anger as you see the place the devil has taken position in the

body of the sick one, and you deal with his position with a real forcefulness.[16]

If people didn't get healed, he was sure to place the blame on the sick. Wigglesworth taught that everyone should be able to control their own healing. He blamed persistent sickness on the individual's own unconfessed sin and lack of faith. He declared, "Is healing for all? It is for all who press right in and get their portions."[17] To one sick woman he barked, "If you'll get rid of your self-righteousness, God will do something for you. Drop the idea that you are so holy that God has got to afflict you. Sin is the cause of your sickness."[18] He also states, "There is a close relationship between sin and sickness . . . but if you will obey God and repent of your sin and quit it, God will meet you, and neither your sickness nor your sin will remain."[19] With no regard for biblical teaching on praying and trusting God's will or God's purposes through physical trials and sanctification from unhealed sickness (Gal 4:13-14; James 1:2-3), Wigglesworth confused and spiritually abused those who were sick and desperate by telling them they were the problem and he was the solution. He was especially aggressive toward anyone who approached him for prayer more than once. One poor man experienced public humiliation when Wigglesworth came to the altar and asked the faith healer to pray for him a second time because he wasn't yet healed. Wigglesworth yelled, "Didn't I pray for you last night? You are full of unbelief, get off this platform."[20] Both his method of placing the blame on hurting people for his own failed healing attempts and his violent antics meant to heal people are still practiced today by many false teachers. Later on in the book, we'll get an up close look at Todd Bentley who, like Wigglesworth, assaults people when praying for their healing.

People merely searching for hope were devastated when men like Wigglesworth humiliated them with his shameful practices. Still, countless modern day Pentecostal and Charismatic preachers ignore the hard

---

[16] Smith Wigglesworth, *Ever Increasing Faith* (Springfield, MO: Gospel Publish-ing House, 1924), 135-36.

[17] Wigglesworth, *Ever Increasing Faith*, 37.

[18] Ibid., 38.

[19] Ibid., 41.

[20] Julian Wilson, *Wigglesworth: The Complete Story* (Tyrone, GA: Authentic Me-dia, 2004), 82-83.

facts of history and consider Wigglesworth a hero of the faith. Regardless of modern sentiment, Wigglesworth was a charlatan who exploited the sick by teaching falsely about salvation, sin, and sickness. His legacy does not represent true Christianity nor the character of biblical leadership.

Not all in this lineage of deception are men. During an era when the women's rights movement was gaining traction, it was the perfect opportunity for a leading lady to take center stage.

Aimee Semple McPherson (1890–1944)

In her day, Sister Aimee was as famous as Babe Ruth. Aimee Semple McPherson loved the spotlight. She was flamboyant, theatrical, ecumenical, and had the talents of today's slickest politicians. Though she fought for many good things like putting Bibles in every grade school and helping the poor in Los Angeles, her flawed teaching set the stage for a whole new wave of confusing doctrines. According to McPherson, speaking in tongues was evidence that a person was a part of the "true church."[21] Furthermore, she built herself up as a holy conduit of God Himself. When on a trip from Ireland to China she alleges that God chose her to change the course of church history by bringing His people back to Scripture. She claimed that God spoke to her directly, saying:

> But behold, even as thou sawest the messenger' of light come forth, even so have I chosen and ordained thee, that thou shouldst go forth, and clear away the debris and contamination, with which they have covered and obscured the light of My Word. I have chosen thee and called thee by name that thou should speak unto My people. Look not upon the pages that contain the theories of men, but upon the burning, flaming words of My Word as revealed and illuminated by the Holy Spirit which I have given unto you.[22]

---

[21] Matthew A. Sutton, *Aimee Semple McPherson and the Resurrection of Christian America* (Cambridge, MA: Harvard University Press, 2007), 41, accessed October 14, 2016, eBook Academic Collection, EBSCOhost.

[22] "A Prophetic Message, Given by Mrs. R. J. Semple, in Belfast, Ireland While en Route to China," *Pentecostal Testimony* 1, no. 5 (July 1, 1910): 12, accessed December 7, 2017, http://ifphc.org/DigitalPublications/USA /Independent/Pentecostal%20Testimony/Unregistered /1910/FPHC/1910_07.pdf. It was common for women to be called by their

Aside from the fact that God chose to speak in the 17th century English used in the King James Bible, there is one important thing to be noted: If God did speak these words to her (which these authors reject as true), the fruit of McPherson's teachings demonstrate she failed in her calling. Instead of pointing people to God's Word and "clearing away the debris and contamination," her life and ministry *became* the debris and contamination.

After being widowed by Robert Semple at the young age of 19, she married an accountant named Harold McPherson and settled down in Providence, Rhode Island. Upon hearing a "voice" telling her to go preach, she abandoned her husband, took her children with her and hit the road to go into ministry. Harold filed for divorce in 1921, citing abandonment.[23] Later in 1931 she married her third husband, actor and womanizer, David Hutton. Due to his scandalous lifestyle, however, the two divorced in 1934. Many grew frustrated with McPherson's poor choices: "The response to the marriage demonstrated at last the limits to her adoring public's tolerance. Her organization lost clergy in local ministries who grew tired of the distractions caused by her decisions."[24] As Noll observed, "Part of the sensation surrounding McPherson's career arose from allegations linking her romantically to other men. Even her death in 1944 was not free from sensation—some ascribing it to a heart attack, others to an overdose of sleeping pills."[25] Sadly, her life does not reflect the message of restoration she claimed as the mark of her authority.

In her final 20 years of life, McPherson made her largest impact on the Christian culture by founding her own denomination. She established the Foursquare Church to preach a version of the Gospel more in line with her own personal theology. The term *Foursquare* represents her belief that Jesus had four ministries that made up the full Gospel—anything less was not the true ministry of Christ in her

---

husband's name; in this case, Robert.

[23] E. L. Blumhofer, "McPherson, Aimee Semple," in *Biographical Dictionary of Evangelicals*, ed. Timothy Larsen, D. W. Bebbington, Mark A. Noll, and Steve Carter (Downers Grove, IL: InterVarsity Press, 2003), 400–404. See also, M. A. Noll, "McPherson, Aimee Semple" in *Who's Who in Christian History*, ed. J. D. Douglas and Philip W. Comfort (Wheaton, IL: Tyndale House, 1992), 445.

[24] Blumhofer, 403.

[25] Noll, "McPherson, Aimee Semple," 445–446.

eyes. The four squares are: (1) Jesus is Savior, (2) Jesus is baptizer (implying that He baptizes people with the Holy Spirit, evidenced with tongues), (3) Jesus is healer (implying that because of the cross, all can receive healing now), and (4) Jesus as coming King.[26] Points two and three are exaggerated theologies that teach healing in this life and tongues are evidence for salvation, which is unbiblical. For example, the Apostle Paul was not healed of his ailments (Gal 4:13–14), he even left one of his closest companions behind who was sick (2 Tim 4:20), and Paul was clear that not everyone would speak in tongues (1 Cor 12:30). For McPherson to claim God gave her special revelation and then go and build a denomination based on her own unbiblical theology closely resembles Joseph Smith's own establishment of Mormonism which was based on personal revelation and miracle confirmation rather than the evolution of a biblically reliable denomination.[27] McPherson's brand of denominationalism reflects a fragmented and exclusivist Gospel message at best and, at worst, another Gospel altogether (Gal 1:6–12).

Like today's faith healers, McPherson was always surrounded by controversy. Aside from her divorces, lavish lifestyle, and public family disputes, she made headlines for other things as well. There was her mysterious disappearance in 1926 that was allegedly linked to an affair, though she claimed she was kidnapped.[28] There were numerous financial controversies caused by her lavish lifestyle which she justified as a type of earthly reward for her supernatural work. She had a chartered plane to ensure she always made it to healing services in style and a large Mediterranean-style villa in Lake Elsinore, California.[29] This excess made her unpopular with the press who criticized the use of church funds to support her extravagant lifestyle. The empire McPherson built became a model for future "prophetesses" looking to profit on a loyal fan base.

---

[26] A full explanation of Foursquare Church doctrine can be obtained at www.foursquare.org.

[27] Miller, *Promise of the Father*, 35.

[28] Cf. Mark Galli and Ted Olsen, *Christians Everyone Should Know* (Nashville, TN: Broadman & Holman, 2000), 198.

[29] "Aimee's Castle" still exists today: "Lake Elsinore: Murrieta Church Leader Buys Famed Evangelist's Retreat," *The Press-Enterprise*, August 1, 2015, accessed October 8, 2016, http://www.pe.com/articles/church-775645-dufresne-lake.html.

McPherson used every available method to make the healing service presentations memorable. She hired a set building team to create an awe-inspiring atmosphere and lined up wheelchairs and crutches along the platform to give the impression that people had been healed. Like a true showman, she built the service to reach a climax to ensure people made emotional responses to be healed, saved, or "filled with the Holy Ghost." Anyone supposedly healed was paraded across platforms and everyone watching was left in awe of her power. McPherson used the media methods of her day to get her message out; even telling those who listened to place their hands on the radio set to receive their healing.[30] Audio recordings of her healing services reveal that her voice tone, rhetoric, service order, and strategies have been mimicked by later mystical-miracle revivalists Kathryn Kuhlman and Benny Hinn.

McPherson's professed power was said to be from God but the evidence of her life demonstrated otherwise. Her life resembled a modern-day tabloid celebrity more than a woman of God. Relying only upon the claims of her healing ministry and supernatural power, McPherson is heralded by many today as a legend in the faith. Students of signs and wonders schools still flock to her gravesite in Glendale, California, to lie on her tombstone and soak in her anointing so they can operate in ministry as she once did.

Kathryn Kuhlman (1907–1976)

Out of all the generals in the charismatic hall of fame, perhaps none are more shrouded in mystery than Kathryn Kuhlman. She was born to Joe and Emma Kuhlman in Concordia, Missouri. Her father became mayor of the small town and achieved his success in the community through old-fashioned hard work. Ironically, he despised preachers, saying they were all "in it for the money."[31] Since papa wasn't going to church, it was the Kuhlman women who would eventually make their way to the altar, and soon, into the spotlight.

---

[30] For an in depth (though favorably biased) look at her contribution to Ameri-can history, see: *American Experience*, season 19, episode 228, "Sister Aimie," direct-ed by Linda Garmon, aired April 2, 2007, on PBS.

[31] Jamie Buckingham, *Daughter of Destiny: The Only Authorized Biography of Kathryn Kuhlman* (Alachua, FL: Bridge Logos, 2008), 21.

Through a series of events Kuhlman was given an opportunity to preach her first sermon in a small town. From this simple beginning she launched her ministry and before long she was holding large services. Eventually in 1935, she pitched her revival tabernacle in Denver, Colorado. After a few years of success, Kuhlman made a critical mistake in her personal life and spent the next three decades reinventing her public image in an attempt to remain a relevant part of the evangelical world.

Kuhlman had developed a ministry partnership at both the tabernacle and on the road with Burroughs Waltrip, a married pastor with whom she was suspected of having an affair. When he divorced his wife and left his two sons in Texas, he asked Kuhlman to marry him, which she did in 1938. As they attempted to forge a life together, Kuhlman soon realized that her power and fame were jeopardized by the public scrutiny over the marriage born out of an alleged affair. She eventually left Burroughs and released a public statement that would spiritualize her decision. Missouri State Historian Amy Collier Artman's in-depth report on Kuhlman's public image provides a glimpse of her effort to recover from the Burroughs debacle:

> In a masterful reinterpretation of her life, Kuhlman chose instead to present in speech and print her decision to leave Waltrip as a difficult moment of submission, the yielding of a strong-willed woman to the relentless call of God on her life. In one particularly emotional message given toward the end of her life and captured on the recording titled, *An Hour with Kathryn Kuhlman*, she recounted her decision to leave Burroughs Waltrip:

> I can remember the day, I can remember the hour . . . At 4:00 PM on that Saturday afternoon, on a dead-end street, I surrendered everything . . . It was all settled. [The Holy Spirit] and I made each other promises . . . I spoke in an unknown tongue as he took every part of me. I surrendered everything. Then, for the first time, I realized what it meant to have power.

> Kuhlman ended her story with the words, "That afternoon, Kathryn Kuhlman died."

> Kuhlman's presentation of her "death to self" was simultaneously a powerful image of sacrificial submission and a brilliant manipulation of her identity. If the divorced Kathryn Kuhlman was dead,

then critics had little to work with. As she told it, she was no longer the disgraced divorcee, but a chastened, sanctified, and consecrated vessel for God's Holy Spirit. With this reinterpretation of her persona, she was able to move beyond what should have been a career-ending mistake and even turn it to her own benefit.[32]

Few in Kuhlman's day could pack a stadium with onlookers, provide entertaining music and displays of the miraculous, while keeping the audience balanced with the right amount of laughter and tears. To her credit, she did not preach some of the heretical doctrines embraced by others of her time. Rather, she left her mark as a feminist entrepreneur—a product of her day and age. In a time when women were fighting for equality, her ministry primarily put on a show, taught an over-exaggerated view on healing, and sprinkled in a basic Gospel presentation with an altar call. Beyond all of those elements, the climax was always the offering. Money came pouring in the way it always does in healing ministries because people assume (and are taught) that if they give to God, He'll give them what they want.

Kuhlman loved expensive things and would often spend thousands of dollars shopping on Wilshire Boulevard in Beverly Hills, California.[33] This area in Southern California became one of my favorite places to shop when I [Costi] was working in the elite circles of prosperity gospel preaching. It wasn't uncommon for even my undershirts to be Versace. Money was no object when a suit could cost $10,000, and jewelry was diamond crusted in every detail.

Kuhlman fit the Hollywood scene quite well; complete with an adulterous scandal and lavish wealth. The only difference between her and Hollywood stars was that she was funding her moneymaking strategy in the healing ministry rather than film. Despite claims from her supporters today, history demonstrates she was more of a celebrity than a servant; more of an actress than an anointed woman of God. During her public ministry, she was not fully trusted by many charismatic leaders and Holiness-Pentecostals because she never publicly demonstrated the ability to speak in tongues and refused to allow tongues-speaking in her services.[34]

---

[32] Amy Collier Artman, "Protecting Her Image: Kathryn Kuhlman and the Manipulation of Negation," *Bulletin for the Study of Religion* 43, no. 2 (April 2014): 20.

[33] Buckingham, *Daughter of Destiny*, 262.

Beyond all of the controversy surrounding Kuhlman's personal life, perhaps nothing has raised more concern than the documented research on her healing ministry. Controversy erupted when a well-meaning doctor conducted a study to verify some of the healings Kuhlman claimed had occurred in her meetings. Dr. William Nolen studied 25 people who had been declared healed at one of Kuhlman's crusades in Minneapolis, Minnesota. [35] The results did not verify Kuhlman's claims. Two specific examples best illustrate the common embellishments and exaggerations that have become a mainstay in the modern healing movement. One woman in Dr. Nolen's study was announced by Kuhlman as having been healed of lung cancer, but later it was confirmed the woman actually had Hodgkin's disease and was not healed. Another woman with a cancerous vertebrae tossed aside her braces and ran across the stage on Kuhlman's command. The crowd roared and Kuhlman gushed with joy. The following day the woman's vertebrae collapsed and four months later she was dead. Still, the question must be asked, how could a woman who claimed to have had personal, audible, verbal communication from God be so unclear when it came to integrity and accuracy in her ministry? Jesus' miracles were irrefutable by even His opponents. Why are faith-healers unable to achieve that same standard?

In the later years it appears that Kuhlman distracted her audience from dwelling on her moral failures, suspect healings, and financial scandals by entertaining them with elaborate stories about her traveling adventures and of unusual (and unverifiable) healings. A simple review of video footage will show that she used endorsements and support from celebrities, politicians, and even Catholic priests to keep herself elevated in the eyes of supporters. Her crusade in Las Vegas on May 3, 1975, serves as a perfect illustration of these PR tactics. When the

---

[34] D. J. Wilson, "Kuhlman, Kathryn," in *Dictionary of Pentecostal and Charismatic Movements*, ed. Stanley M. Burgess, Gary B. McGee, and Patrick H. Alexander, (Grand Rapids, MI: Regency Reference Library, 1988), 529.

[35] Lester Kinsolving, "Kuhlman Tested by MD's Probe," *Pittsburgh Post-Gazette*, November 8, 1975, accessed January 2, 2018, https://news.google.com/newspapers?id=cOQNAAAAIBAJ&sjid=iG0DAAAAIBAJ&dq=kathryn%20kuhlman%20william%20nolen&pg=5280%2C834951.

service structure and strategy is compared to modern day faith healers like Benny Hinn, it is nearly an exact match.[36]

Her ministry was a ladder for fame and power and she climbed high during a time when women were desperate for equality. At best, Kuhlman may fall by God's grace into the category of preaching Jesus Christ based on pretense (Phil 1:18); at worst, she was a woman capitalizing on feminism, the Bible, and desperate people seeking healing so that she could enjoy celebrity stardom and wealth.

William Branham (1909–1965)

When World War II ended in 1945, millions of Americans experienced the aftermath of a difficult six-year global war. Even with the allied victory over the Nazis, the horrific devastation of the war left many people jaded, in a state of shock, and without much hope in humanity. As if on cue, a man rose to prominence offering a form of hope and supernatural deliverance that millions were seeking. His name was William Branham. His legend began from the day he was born—April 6, 1909:

> With the light beginning to break through the early-morning skies, the grandmother decided to open a window so the Branhams could better see their new son. It was then that the first supernatural occurrence happened to young [William] Branham. In his own words, he tells the story as it was described to him:
>
> "Suddenly, a light come whirling through the window, about the size of a pillow, and circled around where I was, and went down on the bed."[37]
>
> Neighbors who witnessed the scene were in awe, wondering what kind of child had been born to the Branhams. As she rubbed his tiny hands, Mrs. Branham had no idea those same hands would

---

[36] "Dry Land Living Water," directed by Kathryn Kuhlman Foundation, featuring Kathryn Kuhlman, aired May 3, 1975, https://youtu.be/K1m770juVuc. While we recognize the impermanent nature of the internet, the nature of this work's topic necessitates the citation of visual sources. If a cited URL no longer works, try a keyword search.

[37] C. Douglas Weaver, *The Healer-Prophet, William Marrion Branham: A Study of the Prophetic in American Pentecostalism* (Macon, GA: Mercer University Press, 1987), 22, as quoted in Liardon, *God's Generals*, 312.

be used by God to heal multitudes and to lead one of the greatest healing revivals to date.[38]

Branham's underdog success story captured the hearts of his audiences wherever he spoke. He presented himself as an innocent baby with a divine calling. Like a rose rising out from the thorns, he was a self-glorified savior who had come from the ashes of a poverty-stricken home with an alcoholic father to fulfill his mission from God. With his claims of direct communication with God Himself, a personal visit to Heaven, bright lights from Heaven shining upon him, and the power to heal all those who were sick and afflicted, Branham's personal testimony was extraordinarily captivating.[39] Perhaps the most heart-stopping story of all was his description of his wife's death from tuberculosis coming on the same night his newborn daughter died during the aftermath of the Great Ohio Flood of 1937. Like the hero in a love story, Branham was separated from his wife who had recently given birth. Through raging floodwaters and the resulting chaos, he would find his bride just in time to hold her for her final breath. Roberts Liardon brings readers to tears as he captures Branham's tragic story:

> Branham grabbed her and shook her, crying, "Honey! Answer me! . . . God, please let her speak to me once more." And suddenly, [his wife] Hope opened her eyes. She tried to reach out to Branham, but she was too weak.
>
> She looked at her husband and whispered, "I was almost home. Why did you call me?" Then in her weak, faltering voice, she began telling Branham about Heaven. She said, "Honey, you've preached it, you've talked of it, but you can't know how glorious it is."
>
> Tearfully, she thanked Branham for being a good husband, and then she began to grow quieter. Branham finishes the story this

---

[38] A portion of this quote is an excerpt from one of Branham's most favorably biased biographies by Roberts Liardon. Much of what is claimed in his biography is unverifiable hearsay littered with spurious details. Liardon, *God's Generals*, 312.

[39] Stephen Hunt, "Deliverance: The Evolution of a Doctrine," *Themelios* 21, no. 1 (1995): 11.

way: "She pulled me down to her and kissed me good-bye. . . .
Then she went to be with God."

. . . Shortly after his prayer, baby Sharon joined her mother in
Heaven.

In just one night, Branham had lost two of the three most
precious people on earth to him. Only Billy Paul was left.

Two days later, a heartbroken man buried his daughter in the
arms of her mother. It seemed his grief was too great to be
endured. Yet, in the coming years, the remembrance of those
feelings would cause the tears of compassion to flood his cheeks as
William Branham prayed for the sick.[40]

With this type of testimony, audiences would melt at the courage
and compassion of this seemingly God-sent messenger. How could they
not accept Branham as trustworthy and anointed by God? Any parent
who loves their children can resonate with Branham's heart-ache.

By the 1950's he had become a household name but controversy
swirled around his ministry from the beginning and his teaching raised
major concerns in the later years. When it comes to Branham's
theology, one needs to look beneath the surface of his emotionally
stirring testimony and claims of healing power to find that he taught
an entirely *other* kind of gospel than the Gospel of Jesus Christ.

Branham's numerous claims about his revelations from God were
blasphemous at best. Preaching one of his most famous series about
the seven seals in the book of Revelation, Branham put his
supernatural revelation of the end times in a category beyond even
Christ Himself:

> Jesus never spoke of it. John couldn't write it. Angels know
> nothing about it. What is it? It's the thing that Jesus said even the
> Angels of heaven didn't know nothing about it. See, see? He
> didn't know it Himself, said only God would know it, but He told
> us when we begin to see these signs coming up . . . (Now, you
> getting somewhere? All right.) Notice, we can see these signs
> coming up. See? If Satan could get a hold of it . . . If you want
> something to happen . . . Now, you'll have to take my word for

---

this. If I'm planning on doing something, I know better than to tell anybody about it. Not that that person will tell it, but Satan will hear it. See? He can't get it in my heart there, as long as God's got it closed up with the Holy Spirit, so it's between me and God. See? He don't know nothing about it until you speak it, then he hears it.[41]

After preaching for over an hour about his supposed revelation from God, Branham elects not to reveal it to his audience who waited patiently for him to back up his claims.[42]

When preaching one Sunday, Branham daringly exclaimed his own idea about the deity of Christ. He declared, "He never died as God. He died as a man."[43] Branham also denied hell was eternal.[44] In another long-winded sermon, Branham suggested that he himself was Elijah, but he never once clarified exactly what he meant.[45] Last but not least, Branham taught the "Serpent-Seed" doctrine which is the belief that Satan seduced Eve into having sexual intercourse and produced Cain, thus infiltrating the human race with his seed.[46]

---

[41] William Branham, "The Seventh Seal" [sermon], Branham Tabernacle, Jeffersonville, IN, March 24, 1963, accessed November 20, 2016, http://branham.ru /message/messageec26.html?sermonum=928.

[42] 1,131 of Branham's sermons have been posted on the Promised Restoration website: http://www.en.branham.ru/index.php.

[43] William Branham, "The Mighty Conqueror" [sermon], Branham Tabernacle, Jeffersonville, IN, Sunday April 1, 1956, accessed November 20, 2016, http://branham.ru/message/message10cf.html?sermonum=309.

[44] Branham on no eternal hell: "The Bible said, 'forever and (conjunction) forever.' Jonah said he was in the belly of the whale forever. It's a space of time. But, look, there's only one Eternal Life, and that's God. And if you're going to be tormented forever and can never die, you got Eternal Life. You can't be tormented forever. You may be tormented for a hundred million years in the Presence of God and the holy Angels, with fire and brimstone. I don't know how long His judgment is. But it's finally got to come to an end, because it had a beginning, and God alone has Eternal Life." William Branham, "Hebrews Chapter Four" [sermon], Branham Tabernacle, Jeffersonville, IN, September 1, 1957, accessed November 20, 2016, http://branham.ru /message/message9dda.asp?sermonum=437.

[45] William Branham, "Trying to Do God a Service Without It Being God's Will" [sermon], Washington Youree Hotel, Shreveport, LA, November 27, 1965, accessed November 20, 2016, http://branham.ru/message/messagee9c1.html ?sermonum=1116.

Perhaps the most eye-opening fact surrounding Branham's ministry is his link to the infamous cult leader, Jim Jones. Jones was a professed Christian preacher who had the same type of faith-healing ministry as Branham. Jones, however, evolved into arguably the most devastating cult leader in US history; responsible for leading a mass suicide in 1978 that tragically resulted in the death of 918 people—including 304 children under the age of 18.[47] An article by John Collins and Peter M. Duyzer on the website, "Alternative Considerations of Jonestown and Peoples Temple," sponsored by the Special Collections of Library and Information Access at San Diego State University, details the connection between Branham and Jones, including that they actually held healing services together:

> In March 1956, when Branham announced a new campaign to be held for four days in June that year, Jones promoted the event through the *Herald of Faith* newsletter, the *Open Door* newsletter, local newspapers and mailing lists. The strategy was successful: Branham's name attracted some eleven thousand people to the Cadle Tabernacle, and the evangelist performed numerous miracles through his alleged gift of discernment which facilitated healing the sick. In the months to follow, Jones too, became a familiar name within the healing revival movement for possessing the same supernatural gifts.[48]

The errors of Branham's teaching and deceptive stories are too many to list here. Just a cursory look at his life and ministry provides clear evidence that he deserves the title *false teacher*. He took biblical

---

[46] Branham on Satan having sex with Eve: "He could not have a child directly by Eve as did God by Mary, so he entered into the serpent and then beguiled Eve. He seduced her and by her did Satan have a child vicariously. Cain bore the full spiritual characteristics of Satan and the animalistic characteristic of the serpent." William Branham, "The Serpent's Seed" [sermon], Branham Tabernacle, Jeffersonville, IN, 1958, accessed November 20, 2016, http://www.en.branham.ru/read_prop.php?date=58-0928E.

[47] 909 people died in Jonestown, five others were shot, and four died at another location.

[48] John Collins and Peter M. Duyzer, "The Intersection of William Branham and Jim Jones," Alternative Considerations of Jonestown & Peoples Temple, last modified October 20, 2014, accessed November 20, 2016, http://jonestown.sdsu.edu/?page_id=61481.

truth, mixed it with error, and poisoned his audiences spiritually. Case in point: Branham's life ended on Christmas Eve 1965 from injuries sustained in a head-on-collision on the night of December 18 and his funeral took place on December 29; however, his cult-like followers delayed his formal burial nearly four months expecting his resurrection.

Branham's life and death marks a unique shift in the post-WWII religious scene. While faith-healing ministries would still be the biggest draw for crowds, the storehouse of wealth available to these generals was still largely untapped. That is until Kenneth Hagin and Oral Roberts began to teach people that God didn't just want them healed and heal-thy, but He also wanted them happy and wealthy. This new money-making strategy was coined, "The Word of Faith" movement and became the forerunner to the full-fledged doctrine of the "Prosperity Gospel."[49]

Oral Roberts (1918–2009)

Granville Oral Roberts pioneered the prosperity gospel and "seed-faith" theology as it is known today. Both of these teachings meant one thing for Roberts—money. Unlike his predecessors, the facts surrounding Roberts' life and ministry are not filled with moral failure and his teachings were crystal-clear to everyone. Born in humble circumstances, the son of a preacher, young Roberts suffered from tuberculosis. At the age of 17 he claimed that God spoke to him personally and healed him. His own biography documents this life-changing moment:

> "Son, I am going to heal you, and you are to take My healing power to your generation. You are to build Me a university based on My authority and on the Holy Spirit." Roberts was miraculously healed that night of both tuberculosis and lifelong stuttering. His call from God and supernatural healing marked the beginning of a miracle ministry.[50]

---

[49] A full history of the Prosperity Gospel is beyond the scope of this book. However, we encourage our readers to explore how the confluence of Pentecostalism, New Thought, and American-pragmatism shaped this uniquely modern theology of wealth in Kate Bowler, *Blessed: A History of the American Prosperity Gospel* (New York: Oxford University Press, 2013).

[50] "Oral and Evelyn Roberts," Richard Roberts, Oral Roberts Ministries, accessed December 23, 2016, http://oralroberts.com/about/our-history/oral-roberts/.

Not long after his dramatic claim of healing, he married Evelyn Lutman Fahnestock on Christmas Day in 1938. Together they developed the theology that bankrolled the family business. History scholar Christopher Reed captures this moment in his obituary of Oral Roberts after his death in 2009:

> At the age of 29, he was a struggling part-time preacher with church pastorates in Oklahoma, and his college studies had not brought him a degree. He told the story of how he picked up his bible and it fell open at the Third Epistle of John. His eye caught verse two, which read: "I wish above all things that thou mayest prosper and be in health, even as thy soul prospereth." He had not heard this verse before and neither had his schoolteacher wife Evelyn, though both were the offspring of preachers. Roberts decided immediately that it was all right to be rich. The next day he bought a Buick and God appeared, he said, telling him to heal people. Roberts then added this aspect to his tent revival meetings and a month later in Enid, Oklahoma, he cured, he said, a woman the use of whose hand had been impaired for 38 years.[51]

Roberts didn't mince words about his version of Jesus or the gospel. He boldly taught and defended his belief that Jesus' highest wish for every believer was to prosper materially and have physical health in this life equal to His peace and power in the soul.[52] Roberts twisted the Bible to make his point: telling his readers that it was Jesus who said in 3 John 1:2, "Beloved, I wish above all things that thou mayest prosper and be in health, even as thy soul prospereth," when in fact that was the Apostle John's loving way of greeting his readers at the time.[53]

Bestselling books by Roberts brought the two distinct teachings of the prosperity gospel and word of faith movement together under one roof. His books included catchy titles such as, *If You Need Healing Do These Things*, *The Miracle of Seed-Faith*, *A Daily Guide to Miracles*, and *Suc-*

---

[51] Christopher Reed, obituary for Oral Roberts, *Guardian*, December 15, 2009, accessed December 23, 2016, https://www.theguardian.com/world/2009/dec/15/oral-roberts-obituary.

[52] Oral Roberts, *If You Need Healing Do These Things* (Garden City, NY: Country Life Press, 1950), 15.

[53] Ibid.

cessful Living through Seed-Faith. Desperate crowds could not resist his big promises and remained unaware, or unconcerned, that Roberts was mishandling the Gospel of Jesus Christ. This new theology of unlimited health and wealth meant big crowds and big money—but big problems were on the horizon.

Roberts didn't just use scripture-twisting tactics to build his prosperity gospel empire into a multi-million-dollar machine. He was incredibly innovative. In 1963, Roberts was able to leverage his Native-American heritage to obtain a United States land-grant for the property on which he would build a university. Oral Roberts University has a 500-acre campus in Tulsa, Oklahoma, with nationally recognized sports teams in the NCAA and draws students from all over the world. Roberts reason for starting the school was based on God's verbal command to, "Raise up students to hear My voice, to go where My light is dim, where My voice is heard small, and My healing power is not known, even to the uttermost bounds of the earth. Their work will exceed yours, and in this I am well pleased."[54]

He also built a faith-healing-based hospital in 1981 called City of Faith. His stated goal was to merge the power of prayer with science and medicine. This towering structure was built through the giving of ministry partners (a mailing list of followers who are committed to Oral Roberts and his mission) who donated $120 million in 4 years. Roberts told his partners about a face-to-face conversation he had with Jesus where he was told the ministry partners would give the money:

> According to the letter forwarded by Thompson, Roberts says he encountered Jesus at 7 p.m. as Roberts stood praying in front of the City of Faith in south Tulsa. He said it was the second time he had met him [sic]. In the letter, Roberts told his partners, "I felt an overwhelming holy presence all around me. When I opened my eyes, there He stood . . . some 900 feet tall, looking at me; His eyes . . . Oh! His eyes! He stood a full 300 feet taller than the 600-foot-tall City of Faith." "There I was face to face with Jesus Christ, the Son of the Living God," Roberts continued. "I have only seen Jesus once before, but here I was face to face with the King of Kings. He stared at me without saying a word; Oh! I will never forget those eyes! And then he reached down, put His hands

---

[54] "Oral and Evelyn Roberts."

under the City of Faith, lifted it, and said to me, 'See how easy it is for me to lift it! Roberts said. Roberts told his partners that he told Jesus he had taken the City of Faith as far as he could. Jesus' reply, according to Roberts, was: "I told you at the beginning that you would not be able to build it yourself [sic] I told you that I would speak to your partners and, through them, I would build it!" Roberts said that Jesus assured Roberts that through the partners the City of Faith would be finished.[55]

Whatever version of Jesus Roberts saw that day, the 900-foot figure had no power to sustain the supposed divinely inspired hospital. The City of Faith lasted 8 years, and every year it was a financial disaster and drain on the university. Roberts tried to recover from his poor business planning by claiming that God said he would end his life if 8 million dollars wasn't raised between January and March of 1987. Worried followers quickly sent in funds and the money was raised. Despite his ability to manipulate the giving of his partners in the short term, the City of Faith was sold to various investors as multi-purpose office space and today is called the CityPlex Towers.

Roberts' teachings and outlandish claims created a legacy built upon a foundation of false teachings. He did not teach about God as described in the Bible. Instead, he developed his own definition of God based on his theology of healing. He wrote,

> If God has ever healed one person, He will heal two, if He heals two, He will heal four, if four then eight and if eight, He will heal all who will believe. Else you make Him have healing compassion for one and not another. Should that be done He would not be God, but a man . . . No, you will not be able to say it is God's will to heal one but it is not His will to heal another—He is either a God of love, perfect love, or He is not God at all. Isn't that right?[56]

Roberts continually rejected God's sovereignty in favor of his own theology of healing. He dismissed God as not being a God of perfect love if He didn't heal everyone. Such a claim is blasphemy against God's perfect nature and His will to glorify Himself through whatever

[55] "Oral Roberts Tells of Talking to 900-Foot Jesus," *Tulsa World*, October 16, 1980, accessed December 23, 2016, http://www.tulsaworld.com/archives/oral-roberts-tells-of-talking-to-foot-jesus/article_bbe49a4e-e441-5424-8fcf-1d49ede6318c.html?

[56] Oral Roberts, *If You Need Healing*, 23.

purpose He decrees (Rom 8:38). God does not promise to heal everyone in this life, yet his love is flawless and his promise of eternal hope remains.

Roberts claimed to have raised dozens from the dead, including a baby in the middle of a service.[57] He taught that salvation and healing in this life were a package deal[58] and that every individual has the power to control their own healing.[59] He also made numerous false prophecies that have been well documented.[60]

By the time Roberts' empire grew to its peak, he was making millions annually and holding up his lifestyle to prove that God was blessing him. In our experience, this is a common strategy employed by prosperity preachers who begin a deceptive cycle by raising riches from their followers, then using those same riches as proof of the legitimacy of their prosperity theology.

Aside from the obvious conclusions one can draw concerning Roberts' credentials as a healer, it may be his lesser-known teachings that inspired much of today's charismatic chaos. He taught seven rules of faith that bring you what you want. Two of them are: "Go where the

---

[57] Associated Press, "Oral Roberts Tells Conference He Has Raised People From the Dead," *New York Times*, June 27, 1987. Richard Roberts (Oral's son) is quoted saying, "Right in the middle of my dad's sermon . . . a woman came running up to the platform with her baby in her arms screaming, 'My baby has just died. My baby has just died.' 'The child had died during the service. My dad had to stop in the middle of his sermon and lay hands on that child. And that child came back to life again.'" Richard Roberts speculated that there were "probably dozens and dozens and dozens of documented instances of people who have been raised from the dead." Yet to this day the ministry provides no evidence of these claims.

[58] Roberts, *If You Need Healing*, 29–30.

[59] Ibid., 38. Although there is no direct evidence that Oral Roberts read the works of Thomas Troward, his work on mind science emphasizing the ability of every individual to control their own healing may have been a precursor to Robert's Word of Faith theology. For further study see, Thomas Troward, *The Edinburgh Lectures on Mental Science*, rev. and enl. ed. (London: Stead, 1909).

[60] Phillip Johnson, "Rubber Prophecies," Pyromaniacs Blog, posted November 4, 2005, accessed December 23, 2016, http://phillipjohnson.blogspot.com/2005/11/rubber-prophecies.html. In this post Johnson documents false prophecies by Roberts and the way modern prophets "reinterpret, twist, and radically reshape their own prophecies in their blind desperation to manufacture 'fulfillments' for bogus forecasts."

power is" and "Lose yourself."[61] These two rules have proven to be some of the most dangerous advice any teacher can give. Today, millions flock to false teachers and mystical-miracle compounds like Bethel Church in Redding, CA. Organizations like their School of Supernatural Ministry are powered by urging young adults to flock to Redding to receive special powers and anointing.

Kenneth Hagin (1917–2003)

Kenneth Hagin is widely known as the "Father of the Word of Faith" movement and has influenced today's richest preachers in countless ways. Hagin, like every other general, claimed his teachings came directly from God as a divine revelation. He taught that God gave every individual the power to achieve great things if only they would confess it out loud. The "Word of Faith" belief system is a popular type of theology that tells people they can get healing, money, jobs, babies, and more, but they must speak these things into existence by faith.

Though Hagin has received significant credit for spreading this "name it and claim it" version of Christianity, this corrupt theology came, in part, from his predecessor E. W. Kenyon. Long before televangelists were filling the airwaves with expensive suits and moneymaking promises, E. W. Kenyon developed a new cultish-hybrid theology at the turn of the 20th century. "What I confess, I possess," he declared, as he mixed the beliefs of Phineas P. Quimby's hypnotizing New Thought teachings with Christian teachings.[62] Quimby's metaphysical philosophy taught that humans can use the mind to alter reality with the power of confession. The problem with Kenyon's theology was that he changed biblical confession from its focus on sin, faith, and right belief about Jesus Christ (Rom 10:9; 1 John 1:9) and instead taught people to confess their desire for temporal comforts—like healing and material prosperity. According to Kenyon:

> God never planned that we should live in poverty, either physical, mental, or spiritual. He made Israel the head of the nations financially. When we go into partnership with Him, and we learn His ways of doing business, we cannot be failures . . . He will give you

---

[61] Roberts, *If You Need Healing*, 73.

[62] E. W. Kenyon, quoted in Simon Coleman, *The Globalization of Charismatic Christianity* (Cambridge, UK: Cambridge University Press, 2000), 45.

the ability to make your life a success.[63]

Much of what Kenyon taught sounds like a transcript from a sermon by the famed televangelist Joel Osteen.[64] This similarity is probably because Osteen was indirectly influenced by Kenyon's teachings as he grew up in a Word of Faith household under his father, John Osteen—who was the pastor of the church Joel now leads. The following quote by E. W. Kenyon sounds like one of Osteen's television sermons: "You will seldom rise above your words. If you talk sickness you will go to the level of your conversation. If you talk weakness and failure you will act it. You keep saying, 'I can't get work,' or 'I can't do this,' and your words react to your body."[65] Kenyon also taught, "Confession always goes ahead of healing. Don't watch symptoms, watch the word, and be sure that your confession is bold and vigorous."[66] When discerning how to view this type of teaching, one must consider that Mary Baker Eddy used New Thought teaching as a building block when she developed the Christian Science cult. Kenneth Hagin comes from this family-tree of theology.

To build his platform of power, Hagin used a dramatic conversion story filled with fantastical claims of supernatural experience. At age 15 he was dying of heart problems. After a supernatural visit to hell on three separate occasions and one trip into glory,[67] Hagin returned to his body and recovered from his disease. Before launching his ministry, Hagin claimed that Jesus personally appeared to him eight times (after his trip to hell) over the course of several years.[68]

---

[63] E. W. Kenyon, quoted in Dale H. Simmons, *E. W. Kenyon and the Postbellum Pursuit of Peace, Power, and Plenty* (Lanham, MD: Scarecrow, 1997), 246.

[64] Remarkably, in our receipt of email correspondence from around the world, the two names mentioned in *every* country, including closed nations, are Joel Osteen and Bill Johnson.

[65] E. W. Kenyon, quoted in Simmons, *E. W. Kenyon*, 172.

[66] E. W. Kenyon, *Jesus the Healer* (Seattle, WA: Kenyon's Gospel Publishing Society, 1943), 26, quoted in David W. Jones and Russell S. Woodbridge, *Health, Wealth, and Happiness: Has the Prosperity Gospel Overshadowed the Gospel of Christ?* (Grand Rapids, MI: Kregel Publications, 2011), 52.

[67] Kenneth Hagin, *I Went to Hell* (Tulsa, OK: K. Hagin Ministries, 1982), https://jesusaufderstrasse.files.wordpress.com/2014/07/i-went-to-hell-hagin.pdf

[68] "Founders Memorial: Kenneth E. Hagin [and] Oretha Hagin," Kenneth Hagin Ministries, accessed December 26, 2016, http://www.rhema.org/index.php?option=com_content&view=article&id=8&Itemid=137.

After several unsuccessful attempts at pastoring a local church, Hagin left the pastorate and began his itinerate ministry. In 1967, he launched his own radio program. By 1968, Hagin had started his first magazine, *The Word of Faith, which* is still in circulation today. He also founded the Rhema Bible Training College in 1974. The stage was set and his teachings spread like wildfire. Though Kenyon had been dead since 1948, his cultish beliefs and heretical theology lived on posthumously through Hagin.

Hagin was a word of faith specialist but he employed many other methods of teaching that caused the crowds to literally roar. He taught regularly on the "anointing" (a special power given by God to chosen leaders) and grounded much of his teaching on his own personal revelations from God with select Bible verses sprinkled in. His services were filled with demonic-like behavior and false teaching. A video posted on YouTube titled, "Kenneth Hagin Pretends He Is About To Preach; Acts Demon-Possessed Instead," captures our claim perfectly. In this video, Hagin is preaching to thousands, then gives up on preaching his sermon and begins to laugh wickedly. Upon leaving the platform mid-sermon, footage captures him walking through the crowds—flickering his tongue like a snake. He shouts, "Drunk again!" while people convulse, scream hysterically, and fall to the ground.[69] While this practice was given by Hagin as evidence for being "drunk in the spirit," it is really an indication of the biblical illiteracy of so many in the church. Bizarre experiences, like those seen on video, provide just a small sampling of the aberrant and demonic behaviors exhibited in these services.

Contrary to what we read in Hebrews 9:22, Hagin insisted that Jesus' shed blood on the cross was insufficient for mankind's salvation and that Jesus himself had to be born again. To satisfy Hagin's own version of the Gospel, he taught that Jesus took upon himself Satan's nature through "spiritual death." He taught, "Physical death would not remove our sins. He [Jesus] tasted death for every man—spiritual death. Jesus is the first person ever to be born again. Why did HIS [sic] spirit need to be born again? Because it was estranged from God."[70] Hagin continues, "spiritual death also means having Satan's nature."[71]

---

[69] Phil Johnson, "Kenneth Hagin Pretends He Is About To Preach; Acts Demon-Possessed Instead" [video], posted November 2014, accessed December 26, 2016, https://youtu.be/o7A_1JuHLHs.

Hagin also taught that Jesus was not the only begotten son of God until He was born again in hell and resurrected. In outright contradiction to the clear teaching of John 3:16, Hagin claimed,

> No, 'thou are my son, this day have I begotten thee' is not talking about the day He [Jesus] took upon Himself a body. Then what day was it? When was it that Jesus was begotten? When He was raised up. On that Resurrection morn! Why did He need to be begotten or born? Because He became like we were, separated from God. Because He tasted death for every man, His spirit, His Inner man, went to hell in our place.[72]

All false teaching is deadly but perhaps nothing Hagin taught was more openly blasphemous than his "little god" theology. This heresy teaches people to elevate their view of themselves; that they too are a god. The teaching is unbiblical and contrary to what the church has accepted for 2,000 years.[73] Hagin wrote, "The believer is as much an incarnation as was Jesus of Nazareth."[74] He taught that each person was "created on terms of equality with God, and he could stand in God's presence without any consciousness of inferiority . . . God has made us as much like Himself as possible . . . He made us the same class of being that He is Himself!"[75]

Though many Christians were equipped to spot the errors in his work, the truth about Hagin's ministry only became visible to some near the end of his life when he was exposed as a fraud. In addition to his unbiblical teaching, countless writings were plagiarized. Several years before Hagin's death, D. R. McConnell, who did graduate work at Oral Roberts University, published verified evidence that Hagin plagiarized the work of E. W. Kenyon.[76] Interestingly, Hagin often

---

[70] Kenneth Hagin, *The Name of Jesus* (Tulsa, OK: Kenneth Hagin Ministries, 2007), 29–30.

[71] Ibid., 31.

[72] Ibid., 29.

[73] Scott Newman, "The Appeal of God's Truth to the Mind: Theological and Exegetical Answers to Post-Modern Trends within Evangelical Thought," *Conservative Theological Journal* 1, no. 2 (1997): 142.

[74] Kenneth Hagin, "The Incarnation," *Word of Faith* 13, no. 12 (December 1980): 14.

[75] Kenneth Hagin, *Zoe: The God Kind of Life* (Tulsa, OK: Kenneth Hagin Ministries, 1989), 35–36, 41.

referred to Kenyon's work as direct revelations from God.[77] Kenyon's daughter chose to speak up publicly about Hagin plagiarizing her late father's work (which we also deem heretical). In a taped interview Ruth Kenyon (now Houseworth) explained that Word of Faith teachers "all copied from my Dad" [E. W. Kenyon].[78] Regardless of Hagin's motivations for passing off Kenyon's work as divine revelation, his plagiarism is clear evidence that his ministry was based upon deceit.

Kenneth Hagin's life and ministry were built on a foundation of sand; unfortunately, many preachers influenced by his ministry are happy to copy his theology if it means they can attract large donations. Joel Osteen's use of positive confession is as foundational to his ministry as it was for his dad, John Osteen. John was a proud partner with Kenneth Hagin in making positive confession theology a formative part of the Osteen family legacy.[79]

---

[76] D. R. McConnell, *A Different Gospel: A Historical and Biblical Analysis of the Modern Faith Movement*, rev. ed. (Peabody, MA: Hendrickson Publishers, 1995). In this work McConnell does an outstanding job placing numerous columns of Kenyon's work side-by-side with Hagin's. The results are a shockingly, in most cases a word for word match, as though Hagin (and his editors) copy and pasted Kenyon's teachings and revelations right into his books.

[77] In the preface to his book *The Name of Jesus*, Hagin writes, "I was amazed by how little material there is in print on this subject. The only good book devoted entirely to it was E. W. Kenyon's, *The Wonderful Name of Jesus*. It is a marvelous book. *It is revelation knowledge. It is the Word of God*" [emphasis added].

[78] D. R. McConnell, *A Different Gospel: A Historical and Biblical Analysis of the Modern Faith Movement*, rev. ed. (Peabody, MA: Hendrickson Publishers, 1995), 3–5. McConnell lays out Ruth Kenyon Houseworth's position on those who plagiarized her father's teachings in chapter 1 of this book. He quotes her from the taped interview she did on February 19, 1982.

[79] John Osteen is quoted saying, "I think brother Hagin is chosen of God and stands in the forefront of the message of faith." John Osteen, taped phone interview, Pastor of Lakewood Outreach Center, Houston, TX, February 24, 1982, quoted in McConnell, 4. It is important to note that the influence of this false gospel has spread into outside of Christianity into business and politics. The writings of Norman Vincent Peale, a Methodist preacher, authored titles such as *The Power of Positive Thinking The Positive Principle Today*, and *Enthusiasm Makes the Difference* (which incidentally were criticized for utilizing hypnotic suggestion as we argue later in this book is the case for much of the prosperity-gospel techniques). Peale's influence is felt today; he pastored Marble Collegiate Church in Manhattan which was attended by President Donald Trump and where he officiated the marriage between Trump and his first wife Ivana in 1977. See, Jeet

Conclusion

There are many names enshrined in the mystical-miracle movement's hall of fame. If he completes the project, Bill Johnson's infamous Hall of Generals will certainly showcase many (if not all) of the people included in this chapter as well as many more. By and large the men and women surveyed in this chapter: Charles F. Parham, William Seymour, Smith Wigglesworth, Aimee Semple McPherson, Kathryn Kuhlman, William Branham, Oral Roberts, and Kenneth Hagin are the ones who paved the way for the current generation of Third Wave/NAR leadership.

Heading into the decade of the 1990's, there was trouble in the signs and wonders paradise, as many Bible-believing Pentecostals called out error and split from their former colleagues. In the next chapter we will discuss the late century rupture between historic Pentecostalism and the growing Third Wave/NAR movement. First, some final remarks:

It's important to understand that what you've just read is the heart-breaking lineage behind the mystical-miracle veil. After I [Costi] was saved from this deception, I began to devour sound biblical teaching and study church history (and that helped), but it was the relationships in my life that opened the door for discipleship. I needed help—and many Christians were there for me. Day after day I discovered just how wide the divide was between what the Bible teaches and what I had been taught, and day after day I discovered how many brothers and sisters in Christ I truly had. This epiphany sent me into nearly two years of what a dear friend calls "Charismatic PTSD." My friend coined the phrase because he's a military veteran who has experienced the challenge of adjusting to civilian life after warfare. He's also a former security guard for a famous faith healer who has experienced the challenge of adjusting to life after witnessing things few would ever believe. After being chewed up by false teaching celebrities, and saved by grace, he spent almost twenty years in confusion and frustration after feeling like he could not trust anyone. He hadn't met many people who could understand what he had

---

Heer, "The Power of Negative Thinking," *New Republic*, October 16, 2017, accessed January 2, 2018, https://newrepublic.com/article/145311/power-negative-thinking-trump-lessons-democrats.

witnessed. When he and I met for the first time, this muscle-bound warrior wept as he explained that he hadn't found the same support or understanding within the church that I was fortunate enough to have had. Few people realized the devastation he had been through and the discipleship that he needed.

This serves as a great reminder that as Christians we have a lot of work to do. At times, we can all be oblivious to the spiritual causalities around us and fail to realize that people need life-on-life support. Like any new convert, people saved out of deception need to be equipped to face the challenging road ahead and be encouraged that there is hope for a new future because they are a new creation in Christ. Many don't know what the Bible teaches or how to start reading it properly, so personal discipleship becomes imperative. At the same time, like people who have been spiritually abused, people saved out of deception need to be loved and supported through the ups and downs of recovery because God isn't finished with them. Instead of falling prey to feelings, they should be encouraged to look at the objectivity of Scripture, while also being assured that emotions are not irrelevant. The emotions that a person may feel when coming face to face with being deceived are real, and they must be dealt with biblically. When we are deceived by those that we trust and love, it is completely normal to experience everything from anger, bitterness, rejection, hopelessness, depression, and suicidal thoughts. Even still, the power of the true gospel and the unstoppable grace of God are enough to heal even the most wounded heart. Where deception has wounded, grace and the power of the Holy Spirit abound much more!

If you're a Christian, determine to view chapters such as these not as historical trash-talking or an "I told you so" moment to shove in the face of friends and family who revere these divergent leaders. Rather, may it be a sobering reminder of how our adversary, Satan, is using false teachers and error to devour those whom we love so dearly. Christian brothers and sisters, arm yourselves with truth and love. The gospel is on the line.

Therefore, laying aside falsehood, speak truth each one of you with his neighbor, for we are members of one another. Be angry, and yet do not sin; do not let the sun go down on your anger, and do not give the devil an opportunity. He who steals must steal no longer; but rather he must labor, performing with his own hands what is good, so that he will have something to share with one who has need. Let no unwholesome word proceed from your mouth, but only such a word as is good for edification according to the need of the moment, so that it will give grace to those who hear. Do not grieve the Holy Spirit of God, by whom you were sealed for the day of redemption. Let all bitterness and wrath and anger and clamor and slander be put away from you, along with all malice. Be kind to one another, tender-hearted, forgiving each other, just as God in Christ also has forgiven you. (Eph 4:25–32)

3

Rupture in the Third Wave

Introduction

The last thirty years of the Pentecostal/Charismatic movement have been embroiled in controversy and church splits. This prompts us to focus on just two of the most influential factions. One faction unsuccessfully attempted to bring back the glory days of Pentecost while the second established a new group called the New Apostolic Reformation (NAR).

Third Wave is a phrase often used to identify the most recent iteration of neo-Pentecostal history spanning the past thirty years. This chapter includes a brief review of Third Wave history in order to provide clarity for the reader. Though there are many subgroups within the various movements that have influenced Third Wave theology, most historians agree on the following general timeline. Lastly, it is our understanding that entire volumes of books can be written on each of these sections and we have only offered a short synopsis. The reader is encouraged to further their understanding of these movements with reputable works on church history.

Early Pentecostalism (Late 1800's to early 1900's)

The Pentecostal theology emphasizing a post-salvation experience of Baptism in the Holy Spirit evidenced by the speaking in tongues was unique to the early 20th century, but finds its roots in the holiness movements of the late 19th century. Early Pentecostals were inspired by John Wesley's (1703–1791) 18th century gospel-centered passion and John Fletcher's (1729–1785) pursuit of Pentecost experience.[1]

---

[1] Eddie L. Hyatt, *2000 Years of Charismatic History* (Lake Mary, FL: Charisma House, 2002), 106.

Wesley's teaching sparked revival in both England and America and formed the foundation for Methodism. Fletcher's teaching helped inspire the men and women of the various holiness movements who were committed to righteous living and the pursuit of Christian perfection through the power of the Holy Spirit. Adapting the often loose terminology of the holiness movements and integrating some of the heretical theology of Edward Irving and Joseph Smith, Charles Parham (discussed in the previous chapter) laid aside the emphasis of holiness, broke from biblical authority, rejected Methodist accountability, and created his own brand of Pentecostalism—giving way to the faith healers and rogue preachers of the 20th century.[2]

Charismatic Renewal (Mid 1960's–1980's)

Centered on the *charismata* (literally meaning: "grace gifts"), this era ushered in a new desire for Spirit Baptism that could be accompanied by many different signs and wonders beyond the Pentecostal expectation of speaking in tongues. On August 3, 1960, news stations began to report about a strange phenomenon out of Van Nuys, CA. Dennis Bennett, an Episcopal priest, claimed to be Baptized in the Holy Spirit and started speaking in tongues. Hysteria spread and soon after reports spread that two thousand Episcopalians were apparently speaking in tongues in Southern California.[3] In the words of one charismatic historian, "The Charismatic Renewal had begun."[4] Other denominations soon began their own pursuit of the same experience and even Roman Catholics held their own conference in 1972 which attracted thirty thousand Roman Catholic Charismatics.[5]

---

[2] A full discussion of the influences behind Parham's unique Pentecostal theology are beyond the scope of this work. For a more thorough survey see, Miller, *Promise of the Father*. For a biblical exposition of how the theology of Spirit Baptism was changed through these various movements, see Miller, *Have You Not Yet Received the Spirit?*

[3] D. W. Dorries, "Bennett, Dennis," in *Biographical Dictionary of Evangelicals*, ed. by Timothy Larsen et al. (Downers Grove, IL: InterVarsity Press, 2003), 44; and Frank Farrell, "Outburst of Tongues: The New Penetration," *Christianity Today* 7, no. 24 (September 13, 1963): 3.

[4] Hyatt, *2000 Years of Charismatic History*, 175.

[5] Hyatt, *2000 Years of Charismatic History*, 178. See also, "The Catholic Charismatic Renewal," Catholic Charismatic Renewal Golden Jubilee, accessed December 6, 2017, http://www.ccrgoldenjubilee2017.org/history.php?lang=en. Further,

Denominational lines blurred as many evangelicals accepted various manifestations of the Spirit as a sign of God's salvation and special blessing.

The Third Wave (1983–Present Day)

In the early 1980's C. Peter Wagner (1930–2016) was a professor at Fuller Theological Seminary who believed modern day signs and won-ders could be wielded by all Christians. He helped design a course at Fuller called, "Signs and Wonders" (course code: MC510)[6] and taught this with his friend John Wimber (1937–1997). It was during this time, at the pinnacle of the Charismatic Renewal era, that Wagner coined the term "Third Wave" as the next big thing to hit the church.

Initially, the Third Wave rejected certain excesses and unbiblical teachings (like tongues as evidence for salvation), and believed that people could stay in their denominations, respect their congregational governance, but still enjoy the work of the Holy Spirit through charismatic-like experiences such as tongues, euphoria, being slain in the spirit, healing power, prophecy, and more. Though walking a fine line for even open-minded evangelicals, and clearly crossing the line for conservatives, initial proponents of the Third Wave were somewhat sober-minded compared to much of what we see in the movement today. In his entry on the Third Wave in the *Dictionary of Pentecostal and Charismatic Movements*, C. Peter Wagner included a list of what movement leaders originally taught—a list that could pass the doctrinal muster of many conservative evangelicals today:

1. "The Baptism of the Holy Spirit occurs at conversion (1 Cor. 12:13)" and is not "a second work of grace."
2. There is one baptism (new birth) but there can be "multiple fillings."

Brian Smith, "The Humble Beginnings of ICCRS," International Catholic Charismatic Renewal Services, accessed December 6, 2017, http://www.iccrs.org/en/about-iccrs/.

[6] C. Peter Wagner, "Wimber, John," in *Dictionary of Pentecostal and Charismatic Movements*, ed. Stanley M. Burgess, Gary B. McGee, and Patrick H. Alexander (Grand Rapids, MI: Zondervan, 1988), 889.

3. God gives tongues to some but not all believers and is not a "validation of [some] spiritual experience but rather a gift" to be used for ministry or prayer.
4. "Ministry is . . . commonly a body of believers rather than individual activities [like that] of a faith healer."
5. Rejection of terms "charismatic" or "Spirit-filled" "because of their alleged implication[s] that those . . . labelled" with these terms are an elite spiritual class. [7]

By and large, it appears that Wagner and Wimber started off with a dream to recapture the early experiences that accompanied the apostles at Pentecost, all the while hoping to bring order to the unbiblical mayhem that had swept through Charismatic Renewal. However, as has happened throughout church history, rebuilding a home on the same faulty foundation only delays the impending collapse. Sadly, the dream of unity built around experience wasn't meant to be and the two men ended up on opposite sides of their own Third Wave dream.

Wimber vs. Wagner: Defining the Difference

John Wimber

At this point in the chapter it's best to employ the wisdom of Solomon, "The wisdom of the prudent is to discern his way" (Prov 14:8a)—stick to the historical facts as much as possible, and be prudent to lay aside personal attack or over-exaggeration. Though still a controversial figure, John Wimber is best known as the beloved founder of the Vineyard Association of Churches, but many remain unaware of some of his questionable theology. [8] While many disagree with Wimber's pro-

---

[7] C. Peter Wagner, "Third Wave," in *Dictionary of Pentecostal and Charismatic Movements*, ed. Stanley M. Burgess, Gary B. McGee, and Patrick H. Alexander (Grand Rapids, MI: Zondervan, 1988), 843-44. Regarding Third Wave, John Piper wrote an interesting article in 1990 about the movement worth noting: John Piper, "The California Conference on Holiness: Kudos and Cautions," Desiring God, February 19, 1990, accessed April 27, 2017, http://www.desiringgod.org/articles/the-california-conference-on-holiness-kudos-and-cautions.

[8] In this chapter, our statements regarding the validity of John Wimber's ministry and/or his Vineyard Association of Churches are formed by empirical data for the purpose of "balanced reporting" regarding Third Wave/NAR

charismatic and kingdom theologies, he vehemently stood against much of what the Third Wave/NAR teach today. Wimber was widely known for the following viewpoints:

1. He stood against the Word of Faith and Prosperity Gospel.
2. He was complementarian (non-ordination of women).
3. He openly acknowledged that he suffered from depression and cancer and rightly condemned teaching that physical healing is guaranteed in this life to all Christians in exchange for their faith.[9]
4. He preached against money hungry faith healers and called their manipulation of people, "religion at its worst."[10]
5. He was known to tell people to stop faking their shaking and excessive manifestations at meetings.
6. During the 1994 Toronto Blessing Revival, he personally flew to Canada and dismissed the Toronto Airport Church from the Vineyard Association of Churches for insane behaviors (including false prophecies, barking like dogs,[11] and acting drunk).[12]

Evidence suggests Wimber served as an example of a more biblically responsive neo-Pentecostalism. Noted theologian Wayne Grudem wrote a response to the critique found in the book *Power Religion* by D. A. Carson, James Montgomery Boice, and John H. Armstrong. In his position paper, Grudem attempted to clear the air surrounding Wimber's teaching. Grudem demonstrates that most of what Wimber wrote and preached had more to do with suffering, the

---

adherents. In no way does this delineation represent our agreement with any stated doctrinal or philosophical positions.

[9] John Wimber, "Signs, Wonders, and Cancer," *Christianity Today*, October 7, 1996, accessed April 28, 2017, http://www.christianitytoday.com/ct/1996/october7/6tb049.html.

[10] John Wimber and Kevin Springer, *Power Healing* (San Francisco, CA: Harper & Row, 1987), 40, 223.

[11] "Toronto Blessing-Brute Beast Mocking the Lord," posted May 16, 2014, accessed February 1, 2018, https://youtu.be/_wZCifteHtc. Grown men are seen barking and crawling on the ground like dogs at the Toronto Blessing.

[12] James A. Beverley, "Vineyard Severs Ties With 'Toronto Blessing' Church," *Christianity Today*, January 8, 1996, accessed April 28, 2017, http://www.christianitytoday.com/ct/1996/january8/6t1066.html.

true gospel, and living for Jesus Christ over any other topic—including spiritual gifts. Any leader or reader choosing to publicly comment on Wimber would be wise to start with Grudem's paper.[13]

Does this mean the history of Vineyard Church is without problems? No. Are there still many excesses that need reform? Certainly. But one thing seems clear, if Wimber had been alive during the past 25 years, he would have stood against the rogue teachings of Bill Johnson, NAR, and what the Third Wave has come to represent. As previously mentioned, mainstream Pentecostal denominations like the Vineyard Association of Churches and the Assemblies of God do not support these divergent movements. This illustrates the reasonableness of asking Pentecostal evangelicals to completely reject the Third Wave's false doctrines and to break ties with false teachers such as Benny Hinn and Bill Johnson.

C. Peter Wagner

C. Peter Wagner, the former Fuller Seminary professor, took the Third Wave movement into a different direction (than his colleague Wimber) when he announced, "The year 2001 [is] the beginning of the second apostolic age."[14] Wagner had founded the New Apostolic Reformation (NAR) during the late 1990's. Its unbiblical vision seeks to restore the office of apostle who takes authority over the church by appointing leaders who will influence world government.[15] He chose the name "reformation" claiming it would be equal in impact to the Protestant Reformation. Some of Wagner's apostolic activities include:

1. Spiritual control of followers as he claims, "NAR apostles receive revelations from God, and consequently they are able to

---

[13] Wayne Grudem, "Power and Truth: A Response to the Critiques of Vineyard Teaching and Practice by D. A. Carson, James Montgomery Boice, and John H. Armstrong in *Power Religion*," Vineyard Position Paper #4, Wayne Grudem.com, March 1993, accessed April 28, 2017, http://www.waynegrudem.com/wp-content/uploads /2012/03/PowerandTruthVineyardPosition Paper.pdf.

[14] C. Peter Wagner, *The Changing Church* (Ventura, CA: Gospel Light, 2004), 9.

[15] For a precise and stimulating explanation of the NAR. see P. J. Hanley, *They Call Themselves Apostles: How Revival Churches Have Been Hijacked by the New Apostolic Reformation* (CreateSpace, 2017).

say 'This is what the Spirit is saying to the churches right now.'"[16]

2. Forming the International Coalition of Apostles and initially charging $69 per month in member dues (in 2000). Later adjusting the fees based on location. International apostles would pay $350 annually, while North American apostles would pay $450 per year or $650 for married apostles.[17]

3. Creating numerous subcategories of unbiblical apostles: you could be a "Vertical apostle," "Horizontal apostle," "Congrega-tional apostle," "Ambassadorial apostle," "Mobilizing apostle," "Territorial apostle," "Marketplace apostle," and more.[18]

Wagner also launched his own training school called The Wagner Leadership Institute. With all this emphasis on creating new apostles through his school, the question we should be asking is this: "Is the idea of creating apostles even biblical?" So before we go any further, let's answer that question.

The Gospels consistently tell us who the twelve apostles were. They were men who knew and saw the resurrected Jesus and were commissioned by him to preach and affirm their message through miracles (Matt 10:2, Luke 6:13; 9:1–10; 17:5). The criteria for apostleship is established in Acts 1:21–22 when another man (Matthias) was chosen to replace Judas, "Therefore it is necessary that of the men who have accompanied us all the time that the Lord Jesus went in and out among us—beginning with the baptism of John until the day that He was taken up from us—one of these *must* become a witness with us of His resurrection."

1 Corinthians 15:4–8 expands on this when Paul writes,

and that He was buried, and that He was raised on the third day according to the Scriptures, and that He appeared to Cephas, then to the twelve. After that He appeared to more than five hundred brethren at one time, most of whom remain until now, but some

---

[16] C. Peter Wagner, *Spheres of Authority: Apostles in Today's Church* (Wagner Publications, 2002), 97.

[17] "Membership Information," International Coalition of Apostolic Leaders, accessed April 28, 2017, http://www.icaleaders.com/membership/.

[18] "Membership Information."

have fallen asleep; then He appeared to James, then to all the apostles; and last of all, as to one untimely born, He appeared to me also.

In this verse Paul connects the appearance of the Lord with his own apostleship and even goes so far to call himself "last of all," clarifying an end to this manifestation and office of apostleship.

Ephesians 2:19-20 provides the historical framework for Paul's definition of apostleship, "So then you are no longer strangers and aliens, but you are fellow citizens with the saints, and are of God's household, having been built on the foundation of the apostles and prophets, Christ Jesus Himself being the cornerstone. . . ." The genitive case here is appositional and can be translated, "built upon the foundation *which is* the apostles and prophets." Thus, the Gospels provide the litmus test for an apostle and Paul calls himself the last apostle and Ephesians 2:20 provides the historical purpose.

Scripturally, apostles were men commissioned by Christ, witnesses of His resurrection, and able to perform miracles (at-will via God's power at their command, not through prayer via God's sovereign choice (Acts 3:6)). Jesus was the Cornerstone of the church, the apostles were the foundation, and all subsequent evangelists and teachers build upon them. Therefore, this special office of apostle was unique to the first century and has ceased.

In contrast to this biblical teaching, Wagner's unaccredited institution promotes the work of one of their doctoral graduates and self-proclaimed linguist, Brian Simmons, who created a unique Bible translation for the NAR. What better way to manipulate and control followers than to have your very own version of the Bible? Mormons and Jehovah Witnesses paved the way for this long before Simmons, but he and the NAR faculty who now lead the Wagner Leadership Institute are following suit. This group claims to bring the emotion back into the Bible by substituting the original New Testament Greek text for Aramaic wherever they deem best and by removing all gender-biased pronouns. The NAR translation isn't just paraphrasing or modernizing the Bible, it's a rewrite that claims to be from God.[19]

---

[19] "FAQ's: Why Another Bible Translation? What Makes The Passion Translation Different Than Other Translations?" The Passion Translation, accessed April 28, 2017, https://www.thepassiontranslation.com/faqs/.

Conclusion

It is essential for the discerning Christian to separate the contributions and ministries of men like John Wimber from those leaders who followed the path blazed by C. Peter Wagner. Different denominations should rightly critique Wimber for any number of his Third Wave errors or missional accolades, but is he a heretic? We would say no. Conversely, C. Peter Wagner embodied the essence of a false teacher and took the Third Wave into an era now being coined the "Fourth Wave."[20] No matter how many waves come, Wagner promoted another gospel and his apostolic mandate has damaged the body of Christ.[21]

John Wimber and C. Peter Wagner both impacted Bethel Church and Bill Johnson, although to varying degrees. Johnson claims Wimber to be the greatest influence on his own mystical-miracle ministry not realizing (or unwilling to admit) Wimber himself decried the very things Johnson says and does! Johnson's connection to Wagner's NAR allows him to teach a course titled "Walking in the Supernatural" at Wagner's Leadership Institute, share the stage with NAR leaders, and share book endorsements with today's top NAR personalities, including but not limited to, Todd Bentley, Randy Clark, Heidi Baker, Che Ahn, John Arnott, Shawn Bolz, and Patricia King.[22]

In one sense, the original Third Wave died with John Wimber. The later developments of the shadowy NAR and "Fourth Wave," have produced a new breed of self-proclaimed apostles, like Bill Johnson, operating in a closed fraternal order outside of denominationalism or accountability structures, and teaching practices far outside the boundaries of even their own Pentecostal and Charismatic forerunners. The next chapter will analyze some of the well-known and less reported conduct of these men and women.

---

[20] James Goll, "The Fourth Great Wave of the Holy Spirit Has Begun," *Charisma News*, accessed December 15, 2018, http://www.charismanews.com/opinion/56670-the-fourth-great-wave-of-the-holy-spirit-has-begun.

[21] Thankfully, the internet provides easy access to information on the New Apostolic Reformation, C. Peter Wagner who founded it, and the self-appointed apostles who lead it today. For numerous encouraging stories from people who have been saved out of this deadly movement, simply search: "Leaving the NAR Church."

[22] See chapter 4 for more information.

4

The Shady World of Stage Sharing

Introduction

Sharing is an essential part of a healthy, united, body of Christ. In fact, more people should try it. In almost every aspect of our lives, sharing is a good thing. If people chose not to share their finances, the church would have no resources to advance the mission. If pastors do not share the truth by teaching sound doctrine, they erode the foundation for evangelism and building a healthy faith community (Rom 10:17). And, if God's people do not share common faith and practice biblical character, we cannot maintain the unity of the Holy Spirit (Eph 5:1-2). Furthermore, it is a great thing when we share the stage to promote missionary efforts and support those who are spreading the gospel. But sharing can turn ugly when leaders don't show discernment with their choice in partnerships. If we are not careful to surround ourselves with people of good moral character, anyone can be misled (1 Cor 15:33). So what can we learn about Bill Johnson from the kind of leaders who share his platform?

As we outlined in the previous chapters, the mystical-miracle movement and leaders like Bill Johnson use the memory of historical figures in the various Pentecostal and faith-healing movements to enhance the status of their own ministries. Johnson's claim of taking on the mantle of leadership from past "generals" of the faith gives him credibility within various denominational circles and links him to the power and anointing from times past. It is a strategy similar to that of a family owned business using the image of their great grandfather to promote the integrity of their modern day product—it's great marketing. But if the corrupt theology from those in Johnson's hall of generals is not enough to establish his lack of discernment, then let's take a look at some of the contemporaries with whom he associates.

Bill Johnson leverages a diverse network of living legends to promote his ministry and establish new territories for his popularity to spread. His network is so intermixed that it is impossible to call it by one name or link it to one type of teaching. It includes those who teach the prosperity gospel, word of faith gospel, and healing gospel. His network also includes those who call themselves modern day apostles and prophets. Being that Johnson is now in his 50's, he has incorporated an intergenerational network of up-and-comers, including his own son Eric who is listed as the co-leader of Bethel Church in Redding.[1] In the following pages, we will look at three disturbing connections in his church and answer some of the most convicting questions about Bill Johnson, the other mystical-miracle leaders, and their shady world of stage sharing.

The Benny Hinn Connection

This section was not easy to write. As the nephew of Benny Hinn, I [Costi] travelled the world with him and many of my family members. But as heart-shattering as it is to see members of my family lead millions into deception, it is equally as motivating when I think of how the power of the true gospel changed my life (Rom 1:16). Let the reader understand fully that anything said publicly in regards to my uncle's life and ministry has already been pleaded privately. For years those closest within the family circle (including my late grandmother who was a believer) begged for the deception to cease. Our differences have not been petty debates over the continuance of certain gifts of the Spirit, but rather over fundamental differences regarding the gospel of Jesus Christ. For the past five years I have had personal conversations with family members who are partnered with Bill Johnson, Bethel Church, Todd White, and the NAR. Some of my own family members have attended their signs and wonders schools and regularly use the Passion Translation, fully convinced that it's the truest revelation we have today. I have made the phone calls, sat in the living room with Bible open, and shouted from the rooftops that we have taught a false gospel and must repent and trust God's grace in spite of our former

---

[1] As a practice, these movements operate more akin to private businesses, rarely assenting to a board of qualified elders for the selection of pastoral position, choosing instead to retain autocratic and nepotistic power in the family.

sins. Much of this to no avail, but God is not done working and neither am I done praying for the Holy Spirit to open their eyes.

God has already saved other Hinn family members. None of them are pastors, but that just means some incredible testimonies are still to come. One of my aunts recently called me and told me, "Keep going Costi! We are proud of you and hope God uses this to save people both inside and outside the family." Another emailed me to say she's been hiding in silence for years; scared to be cast off as a bitter liar because of how she's been treated for questioning certain teachings. But, not every response is so encouraging.

One uncle [not Benny] who believes himself to be an apostle called me and scolded, " I read one of your articles and while I do agree with what you're saying and have thought those things for years, you should never talk about family or oppose family. You are outside of your jurisdiction as a pastor as well [referring to his own authority over me as an apostle]. Do not speak about Uncle Benny, he is the Lord's anointed." You who are reading this may have had similar experiences. Though blood is said to be thicker than water, many of us understand that Christ's blood transcends even the deepest familial bonds.

This book is no smear campaign, nor is it an attempt to trade on the family name. In all seriousness, there isn't much to trade on because it's getting to be old news that Hinn teaches a false gospel. To be perfectly honest, if money-making was the plan, I'd have stuck with the prosperity gospel.

There is no name that matters but one. There is only one name that deserves recognition and only one name that leads to riches— eternal riches. That is the name of Jesus. At His name every knee will bow, and every tongue will confess Jesus as Lord (Phil 2:10-11). Take the name Hinn out of the conversation. Even if my name was Costi Smith, the facts remain the same and Christ remains the Lord. Christians must not stand idly by while God's word is maligned. No matter our attachments and no matter how much we love someone, the most loving thing we can do is tell the truth and stand with Christ. All have sinned and no one is perfect, but those claiming to be teachers are held to a higher standard (James 3:1), and those teaching falsehood about Christ are to be called out (Rom 16:17-18). All of us, every believer, must give an account one day to Jesus and that includes both Anthony and I.

To help remain objective, I've done my best to stick to the facts and offer footnotes to back up any claims. However, I cannot change the fact that I've lived much of what has been written in this book. Therefore, this section contains illustrations from personal experience. These are not meant to be sensationalistic. I accept full responsibility for every word written as one who will give an account to our Lord Jesus.

Toufik Benedictus "Benny" Hinn is an Israeli televangelist who was born in Jaffa, Israel in December 1952. He is known worldwide for large "Miracle Crusades" and a flair the for finer things of life. Hinn, a mainstay in charismatic Third Wave circles for over 40 years, needs little introduction. He is a multi-faceted charismatic leader who can perfectly emulate Kathryn Kuhlman's flair for the dramatic opening of a service. Suddenly, he'll become the spitting image of Oral Roberts—declaring financial prosperity for those who will give him a big donation. Similar to the style of William Branham, Hinn will introduce a new theology that he received directly from God and claim to be a prophet. At any given time throughout his ministry, he has operated as a healer, evangelist, and teacher, as well as a pastor who possesses every gift of the Spirit. Growing up as a reverent follower of my uncle's ministry, I understood that he was never one to stay out of the spotlight of controversy. He is charismatic royalty, and I assumed that people were just attacking him because they were jealous of his blessings and anointing. Therefore, in spite of documented evidence of false healings,[2] ludicrous antics,[3] divorce, and an alleged affair with Paula White,[4] we dismissed these charges by sticking to sentiments like,

---

[2] "Do You Believe in Miracles?" Bob McKeown, *The Fifth Estate*, aired November 3, 2004. This documentary gives irrefutable evidence that Benny Hinn is faking healings.

[3] "Benny Hinn Historic Crusades: Atlanta (2010)," BringBackTheCross, post-ed May 29, 2016, accessed December 12, 2017, https://youtu.be/8kkgccLG1Gg. This Good Friday service took place on April 2, 2010 in Atlanta, GA.

[4] Adrienne S. Gaines, "Benny Hinn Admits 'Friendship' with Paula White but Tells Audience It's Over," *Charisma Magazine*, August 10, 2010, accessed January 6, 2017, http://www.charismamag.com/site-archives/570-news/featured-news/11683-benny-hinn-admits-friendship-with-paula-white-but-tells-tv-audience-its-over. It is worth noting The *National Enquirer* published photos on August 2, 2010, in which Hinn and White are seen holding hands in Rome in July.

"David was anointed and still fell into an affair." Or, "Even the best of men are men at best; look at Peter."

Around the time of my true conversion in 2012, the Hinn family connections grew beyond the usual TBN crowd and linked arms with NAR. Over the past couple of years, my uncle has added one of his most important modern connections to his résumé, namely, Bill Johnson. The reason for this alignment is incredibly important for readers to understand because Johnson and his band Jesus Culture have entered into mainstream evangelicalism. This was something that Uncle Benny could never accomplish on his own. His ministry was widely accepted by Third Wave charismatics and the sick and poor of third world countries, but modern evangelicals had wised up to his antics. Based on what you've read so far, and what is still to come, we will make it clear: But for the v-necks, skinny jeans, and mass millennial following, Bill Johnson is no different than Benny Hinn. It's the same old erroneous theology with a new face.

Johnson and Uncle Benny are similar in their theology and in the manifestations that occur in both of their meetings. A simple search on YouTube will bring you right into the world I grew up in. Common things that occur are people being "slain in the spirit," allegedly healed then testifying on stage, raised from the dead (but never documented), tongues being babbled continually without interpretation, holy laughter, jerking gyrations causing people to shake demonically as they convulse and say, "Whoa," and the declarations of bold prophesies drawing thunderous applause from the hopeful crowds. Does that sound bizarre and unbiblical? That's because it is. Even within my own former ministry circle there were comments made about certain services and manifestations being completely phony. We'd often debrief after the service and compare notes. "That one lady flopping everywhere was definitely of the 'flesh,'" one of us would say, referring to something that *wasn't* of the Holy Spirit. "Yes, but did you see that young man crying as he prophesied? The anointing was all over him," someone else would offer. Looking back, I wince over those conversations. If something was truly of the Holy Spirit, no "debrief" would be needed to determine what was of the flesh and what was of the spirit. Everything done and everything taught would match Scripture.

The Hinn and Johnson ministries are man-made systems full of man-made methods. Yet, for all their similarities there are several differences between Johnson and Uncle Benny (from now on I'll lovingly refer to him as "Hinn" unless I am illustrating).

Johnson is more careful not to flash his wealthy lifestyle and has not (yet) reached the global status enjoyed by Hinn. Johnson appears more approachable because he operates as a local pastor, wears normal clothes, and can't fill stadiums without using his band Jesus Culture to attract Millennials. Hinn, on the other hand, chose to abandon Orlando Christian Center in the 1990's to travel full time and has since packed millions into stadiums because of his charming personality and claims of prophetic revelation. If Johnson has one thing Hinn doesn't, it's the ability to duplicate himself through the thousands of youth who regularly attend his church and his influence over Jesus Culture's massive following. Johnson has built and maintained his growing empire with his theology and through entrepreneurial projects involving music and the arts. Hinn, on the other hand, is a one-man show who built his empire on his personality and dramatic presentation.

Johnson's connection to Hinn is not merely theological, it is familial. While they both have spoken at conferences together,[5] Johnson's connection to Hinn was made through Hinn's eldest daughter and son-in-law.[6] Hinn took notice as Johnson's fame spread and he endorsed Johnson's ministry. With Hinn's global ministry now showing signs of decline, it benefited him to associate with Johnson. Hinn has made, in recent years, several other endorsement deals for the false prophet Manasseh Jordan—whose birth Hinn claims to have prophesied.[7] Jordan

---

[5] "Jesus '16 Bill Johnson 'He is Good,'" Jesus Image TV, December 8, 2016, accessed January 6, 2017, https://youtu.be/5MjSy6H7ovo; and "Jesus '16 Panel," Jesus Image TV, December 9, 2016, accessed January 6, 2017, https://youtu.be/OXPCjeNhWb4.

[6] Koulianos and Johnson minister together. "Michael Koulianos at Jesus Conference 2014," Jesus Image TV, February 25, 2015, accessed January 6, 2017, https://youtu.be/QRQREfLUpdM. Using trendy music and an updated style, Koulianos teaches the same false doctrines that Bill Johnson and Benny Hinn teach.

[7] "Manasseh Jordan Lying Wonder," November 12, 2011, accessed April 7, 2016, https://youtu.be/hKBISUwXoNc. In this video Benny tells the crowd he feels responsible for Jordan, since he prophesied his birth. Subsequent to that por-

claims he's raised someone from the dead for a $2,000 donation,[8] and he continues to bring in millions annually with his prophetic claims. Another big-name preacher Hinn endorsed is Nigerian pastor Chris Oyakhilome[9] who, in classic Benny Hinn-style, dons a white suit[10] and boasts a net worth (est. $30–50 million) similar to that of Hinn.[11] There are millions to be made and so Hinn willingly sets aside any pretense of doctrinal integrity and continues to act as an endorser to these men.

Johnson is The Next Big Thing

Even though Hinn's prophecies have frequently failed to meet the standard of truth, they are proven tools for marketing his ministry. The following is a sample of a 2015 prophecy by Hinn to his studio audience, in which he explains how Johnson will usher in the next big thing and shake America with the fire of revival:

> Bill Johnson is about to shake the United States of America. God's gonna [sic] use Bill Johnson. I've never...I'm gonna [sic] invite him to come with me . . . I've . . . I've . . . I . . . We've never met. But we will. . . . I . . . I repeat about Northern Cal because I don't wanna [sic] nobody to misunderstand what I said earlier. San Francisco I don't see nothin', Oakland, absolutely. San Jose, big time . . . big revival. Sacramento, big revival. Modesto, big revival. And other parts, especially where Bill Johnson's church is . . . massive fire over there.[12]

---

tion of the video, footage captures Jordan at :54 seconds beginning his claim to have raised the dead woman based on the seed of $1000 "sown." Later footage of a different event shows that in which Jordan is telling the same story with different names and monetary amount.

[8] Ibid.

[9] "Pastor Chris Honors Benny Hinn Day 2 at the MHIS," posted November 25, 2016, accessed January 6, 2017, https://youtu.be/N5-kyoL-ycM; and, "Benny Hinn talks about Pastor Chris Oyakhilome," posted October 27, 2016, accessed January 6, 2017, https://youtu.be/WwO-WSwG6Ns. In these videos Chris Okilohome and Benny Hinn exchange honoring endorsements of each other.

[10] "Pastor Chris and Benny Hinn, Final Day, full video (MHIS)," posted November 26, 2016, accessed January 6, 2017, https://youtu.be/fyxAaKqgorU.

[11] Mfonobong Nsehe, "The Five Richest Pastors in Nigeria," *Forbes*, June 27, 2011, accessed January 6, 2017, https://www.forbes.com/sites/mfonobongnsehe/2011/06/07/the-five-richest-pastors-in-nigeria/#509c14626031.

Johnson struck charismatic gold with Hinn's televised endorsement. Since Johnson's theology includes teaching people that they must go wherever revival is happening, prophetic endorsements like Hinn's help fill Johnson's church and his school with people desperate to experience God. Recently, the Jesus Conference held in Orlando, FL, has become the annual gathering of mystical-miracle leaders, including Bill Johnson, Todd White, Benny Hinn, Lou Engle, Reinhard Bonke, and an entire cast of young millennial preachers who emulate these ministries. The conference is coordinated by Hinn's son-in-law.

Hinn is a Verified False Teacher & False Prophet

If we choose to completely overlook Hinn's lifestyle, marital issues, and multi-millionaire-dollar spending from donations made to his ministry as merely issues of human frailty, it wouldn't change his status as a teacher of heretical doctrine. While the media may enjoy spreading juicy gossip about Hinn's slaying of thousands and waving his white jacket, Christians need to focus on examining the evidence of his words. Hinn, like Johnson, is a false teacher.

One example of Hinn's false teaching is his claim that humans are like God. Hinn's "little-god" theology includes calling himself "Benny Jehovah!"[13] He has also revived a gnostic heresy that the Holy 'Trinity' is actually comprised of nine distinct persons; God the Father is three persons, God the Son is three persons, and God the Holy Spirit is three persons.[14] In bold fashion, Hinn has publicly claimed that Jesus, Kathryn Kuhlman, and Elijah have all personally appeared to him in

---

[12] "Benny Hinn, "The Fire of the Holy Spirit is Coming!, October 2015," posted September 3, 2016, accessed January 6, 2017, https://youtu.be/n4Q_oFF9hHM; start at 17:05.

[13] Benny Hinn, Sermon Given at the "Spiritual Warfare Seminar," Jubilee Christian Center, San Jose, CA, May 2, 1990.

[14] Benny Hinn, "A New Spirit," Orlando Christian Center, TBN, aired October 13, 1990. Hinn made an outlandishly heretical statement, "God the Father is a person and He is a triune being by Himself separate from the Son and the Holy Ghost. . . . God the Father is a person, God the Son is a person, God the Spirit is a person, but each of them is a triune being by Himself. If I can shock you, and maybe I should, there are nine of them." See, Benny Hinn, *Good Morning, Holy Spirit* (Nashville, TN: Thomas Nelson Publishers, 1990), 80–92. See also, Hank Hane-graaff, *Christianity in Crisis: The 21st Century* (Nashville, TN: Thomas Nelson, 2012), 145–146.

visions or dreams.[15] Hinn also made headlines when he falsely prophesied that all homosexuals in America will be burned by fire in "about '94 or '95, no later than that."[16] These are a just a few examples of the hundreds of inaccurate teachings and prophesies made by Hinn over the years.[17]

A question I [Costi] am often asked now is how the Hinn family justifies such blatantly false teachings. It is simple: we adapted the doctrine of Total Depravity by twisting it to mean that our special anointing was still corrupted at times by our fallen nature. More commonly, however, we would say that God had changed His mind because people were repenting. These excuses created a moving target for our critics and worked well to alleviate concerns in circles where biblical illiteracy was rampant.

---

[15] Benny Hinn, *This is Your Day*, TBN, aired June 11, 1997. In this telecast Hinn said, "I am standing watching the Lord in this vision heal this man. And now as the man was healed, the Lord looked at me with piercing eyes—I'll not forget that one, I'll tell you. Looked at me with piercing eyes and said, 'Do it'!" Benny Hinn, *This is Your Day*, TBN, aired June 11, 1997. In this portion of his vision Hinn said, "I had a vision of the night . . . I saw myself walk into a room and there stood Kathryn Kuhlman. And I've not seen Kathryn in a dream or a vision [in] years . . . And she said, 'Follow me.' That's all she said. And I followed her to a second room. In that second room stood the Lord." Benny Hinn, Honolulu Miracle Crusade, February 28, 1997. Transcript of Hinn's comments by Mike Oppenheimer, Let Us Reason Ministries, accessed December 15, 2017, http://www.letusreason.org/Pent19.htm. Hinn said, "Can I tell you something? I've never shared this. Never! I was in prayer one day and a man appeared in front of me. It happened for two days in a row . . . He was six feet two. Old man. Had a beard glistening beard. His face was somewhat thin, but very bold! Eyes – crystal blue . . . He looked like a priest. But every part of him glistened like crystal. And I spoke out and I said, 'Lord, who is this man?' Now, I know you may think I've lost my mind, but the Lord said, 'Elijah, the prophet.'"

[16] In a New Year's sermon on December 31, 1989 at Orlando Christian Center, Benny Hinn prophesied, "The Lord also tells me to tell you in the mid-nineties, about '94 or '95, no later than that, God will destroy the homosexual community of America. . . ."

[17] Walter C. Kaiser, Jr., "False Prophet," in *Evangelical Dictionary of Theology*, ed. Walter A. Elwell (Grand Rapids, MI: Baker, 1997), accessed December 7, 2017, https://www.biblestudytools.com/dictionaries/bakers-evangelical-dictionary/false-prophet.html.

Hinn is All About the Benjamins

Hinn has taught false doctrine concerning the Deity of Christ and has blasphemed the Holy Trinity—proving beyond a shadow of a doubt that he is a false teacher. What drives him? From my own personal experience [Costi], the evidence suggests a love of money. In prosperity gospel circles, the love of money is prevalent and such love is unapologetic. It can actually be a form of competition to see who God is blessing the most! One afternoon I will never forget was when my father and I rolled up to uncle Benny's front door in Dana Point, California, in our new Ferrari F430. We told him ahead of time to come out and see what we got. With windows down we laughed as my uncle playfully shouted, "I hate you! I hate you! I hate you!" from his front steps. Although we landed the Ferrari from a shady business deal, it didn't matter. We had won the day because my uncle's Bentley wasn't as expensive as our new toy—God's favor came with 490 hp.

The belief that God wants us healthy and wealthy justifies all sorts of greedy behavior. The lifestyle I lived while growing up in the prosperity gospel was outrageously expensive. It took tens of millions to fund our lavish appetites and *still* put money toward outreach programs and maintain a level of legitimacy. Hinn's love for money and legacy of licentiousness will be immortalized in his statements like this one:

> Make a pledge, make a gift. Because that's the only way you're going to get a miracle. Miracles don't happen when you lay around and say, 'Let me feel something.' Miracles happen when you *do* something, and then you gonna [sic] get it. Then you gonna [sic] feel it . . . As you give, the miracle will begin. Alright, so get to the phones and get busy. . . .[18]

Without question, Christians must consider Johnson and Hinn false teachers—cut from the same cloth—until they publicly repent of their greed and manipulation of people seeking hope.

Jeremiah 29:8–9 serves as a reminder of God's thoughts on those who prophesy falsely when He declares, "For thus says the LORD of hosts, the God of Israel, 'Do not let your prophets who are in your midst and your diviners deceive you, and do not listen to the dreams

---

[18] "Praise-a-thon," TBN, aired November 6, 1990.

which they dream. For they prophesy falsely to you in My name; I have not sent them,' declares the LORD.''

I [Costi] will break form one final time to express that I write this through tears of love for my uncle; I wish desperately that he would run to the grace of God and become a living testimony of true repentance. Even still, if by making such a statement just one reader will consider studying God's word and run away from what they've been taught, this will have all been worth it. My uncle Benny Hinn is no anointed prophet; nor should he be considered a man of God.[19] He is a false teacher who needs to turn from his ways.

Todd Bentley and The Revival Alliance

Growing up in Third Wave charismatic circles, I [Costi] was taught, "Do not ever speak against a man of God." Sometimes this statement is phrased, "Touch not the LORD's anointed!" This is, of course, one of the primary ways of keeping criticism to a minimum and allowing charismatic leaders to cash in and stay credible. It isn't uncommon for someone questioning the unbiblical practices inside these mystical-miracle churches to be threatened with the three C's: cancer, curses, and catastrophic events. Any of these tragedies "may happen to you" if you dare to speak out against an anointed leader. When you are living under a leader who uses these tactics, it feels a lot more like you are a member of the mafia than a biblical ministry. Johnson and Bethel Church use these intimidation tactics to keep people in the revivalist movement from speaking out against the abuses they see first-hand. However, when Todd Bentley's credibility was publicly destroyed, even the mystical-miracle gag-order couldn't stop the truth about other secret sins from being revealed. There was nothing Johnson or any self-acclaimed prophet could do to stop the truth from coming to light.

Prior to 2008, Johnson's friend, ministry partner, and fellow revivalist Todd Bentley had everything going for him. He was the heroic "bad boy" of the signs and wonders movement and was attracting tens of thousands to his meetings across the world. Sporting

---

[19] For a more detailed report on Hinn's life and ministry, Richard Fisher and Kurt Goedelman have written the definitive analysis of the life of Benny Hinn: Richard Fisher and Kurt Goedelman, *The Confusing World of Benny Hinn* (St. Louis, MO: Personal Freedom Outreach, 2013).

a shaved head, chin piercing, long beard, and numerous tattoos, he was a biker turned outlaw preacher. He was raw, uncensored, and refreshingly different from the typical suit-and-tie that appeared in the church pulpits each week. People loved Todd Bentley!

Bentley's prominence peaked in the summer of 2008 when he was "anointed" to lead a gathering in Lakeland, Florida, called the Lakeland Outpouring. At this royal ceremony Bentley received massive endorsements from the biggest names in the charismatic business. A group of famous leaders and self-appointed apostles led by Bill Johnson, Rick Joyner, and C. Peter Wagner laid hands on Bentley to seal his commissioning. Che Ahn, Senior Pastor of HRock and President of Harvest International Ministries, spoke on behalf of the group saying to Bentley, "We recognize that God has chosen you and appointed you to bear much and lasting fruit at this Lakeland Revival . . . knowing that you have walked in a manner worthy of the Lord, pleasing Jesus in every way, bearing fruit and every good work . . . we are here to commission you."[20] They went on to anoint Bentley with special revival oil sent by Chuck Pierce of Glory of Zion Ministries.

Several of the leaders present at this commissioning refer to themselves, then and now, as The Revival Alliance. This alliance is made up six major ministries: Bill and Beni Johnson (Bethel Church), Randy and DeAnne Clark (Global Awakening), Che and Sue Ahn (HRock Church), Rolland and Heidi Baker (Iris Ministry), John and Carol Arnott (Spread the Fire Ministry), and Georgian and Winnie Banov (Global Celebration).[21] The entire event was filmed so potentially millions could watch it unfold, and give their financial support to Bentley.

The revival in Lakeland drew in 400,000 people over the course of three months and aired globally on GODTV. Even with the world-wide coverage, special endorsements, prophetic power, and a supposed impartation from the greatest group of self-appointed prophets in the world, no one predicted what would happen next. In an instant, Bentley's moment in the spotlight dissolved.[22]

---

[20] "Todd Bentley Blessed by Apostles," posted June 25, 2008, accessed April 28, 2017, https://youtu.be/gkrtac7IgXs. This originally aired on GODTV during the Lakeland Revival on June 23, 2008.

[21] See The Revival Alliance website: http://revivalalliance.com for more information.

With over thirty claims of the dead being raised and countless other claims of miracles and healings, ABC News decided to investigate the revival in hopes of finding just one verifiable case to report. Despite Bentley's promise to deliver evidence of the healings, ABC was given no such documentation.[23] After the story of his deception broke, Bentley stepped down from leading the revival and soon after there was news of a scandalous affair with his ministry mistress. In a statement by his board of directors, the following half-truth was offered to the public:

> We wish to acknowledge, however, that since our last statement from the Fresh Fire Board of Directors, we have discovered new information revealing that Todd Bentley has entered into an unhealthy relationship on an emotional level with a female member of his staff. In light of this new information and in consultation with his leaders and advisors, Todd Bentley has agreed to step down from his position on the Board of Directors and to refrain from all public ministry for a season to receive counsel in his personal life.[24]

While this unhealthy relationship was downplayed as being just an emotional one, it was, however, much more, and before long the complete truth came out: Bentley had been involved in a physical affair, left his wife and three children, and married his mistress. Bentley was back in frontline ministry leadership along with his new wife, Jessa, after a brief restoration period led by none other than Rick Joyner.

---

[22] Thomas Lake, "Todd Bentley's Revival in Lakeland Draws 400,000 and Counting," *Tampa Bay Times*, June 29, 2008, accessed February 3, 2017, http://www.tampabay.com/news/religion/todd-bentleys-revival-in-lakeland-draws-400000-and-counting/651191. An archive copy can be found here: https://archive.is/LjCK1.

[23] Jeffrey Kofman, Karson Yiu, and Nicholas Brennan, "Thousands Flock to Revival in Search of Miracles," *ABC News*, July 9, 2008, accessed February 3, 2017, http://abcnews.go.com/Nightline/FaithMatters/story?id=5338963&page=1.

[24] The Fresh Fire Board of Directors, "August 15–From the Board of Directors," Fresh Fire Ministries, August 15, 2008, accessed February 3, 2017, https://web.archive.org/web/20080820120744/http://www.freshfire.ca/printpage_content.php?id=1065.

In a public statement released by Johnson in 2011, he made it clear that he fully endorses Bentley's ministry and the restoration process that took place:

> I recommend Todd to you, believing that you will be blessed and encouraged by his ministry. Perhaps even more important is the fact that Todd will be a reminder to us that it is possible to stand after such a great fall. We all live by grace, and only by grace. We desperately need examples of those who have walked in integrity all of their lives. But when there is sin, we need examples of restoration to bring hope to the broken, many of whom are in our congregations. God will use Todd to be a message of restoration.[25]

Bentley's entire restoration process was an in house project, crafted to show just enough repentance so he could get back into the mystical-miracle game. When these type of scandals happen within the close-knit circles of prosperity-gospel faith healers, it's bad for everyone's bottom line. So what's the best way to spin the PR campaign and get the money rolling in again? Hand select a restoration committee who is highly invested in the leader and their fame, and then dismiss any outside criticism as judgmental, pharisaic behavior. With Bentley's restoration process behind him, he was able to get back to business, and at the same time, make Joyner and Johnson appear like the heroes who saved the day.

If You Can't Heal Em', Beat Em'

Very few ministry methods will make you more (in)famous than bringing back Smith Wigglesworth's violent behavior. That's exactly what Bentley has done—but worse. During a service at the Lakeland Revival, Bentley shared about God's command to beat on a poor old woman in order to heal her:

> I said God, "I've prayed for like, a hundred cripple people, not one [has been healed]?" He said, "That's because I want you to take that cripple ladies' legs and bang them up and down on the

---

[25] Rick Joyner and Bill Johnson, "Update On Todd Bentley—Note from Bill Johnson," Morningstar Ministries, 2011, accessed February 3, 2017, https://www.morningstarministries.org/resources/special-bulletins/2011/update-todd-bentley-note-bill-johnson#.WJT5zIS7d-U.

platform like a baseball bat." [Crowd gasps]. "I walked up and I grabbed her legs and I started going [imitates violent hammer action], 'Be healed! Be healed! . . . I started bangin' em up and down on the platform—she got healed.[26]

Later in the same service, Bentley's violent testimony continued:

And I'm thinking, "God, why is not the power of God moving?" He [God] says, "Because you haven't kicked that woman in the face." [crowd gasps and laughs]. [Bentley continues], "There's this older lady worshipping right in front of the platform and the Holy Spirit spoke to me and the gift of faith came on me and He [Holy Spirit] said, 'Kick her in the face [crowd laughs] . . . with your biker boot.'" [Bentley says], "I inched closer and I went like this, BAM! [kicking motion]. And just as my boot made contact with her nose, she fell under the power of God.[27]

In the same message Bentley describes how a man, hoping for a touch from God, got nothing less than a football tackle and a ground-and-pound beating:

And I saw him and the gift of faith came on me and I said, "What do I do God?" and God told me to just, "Run him down." [Bentley continues,] "So I jumped up in the air and went, 'POW!' and I hit the ground, jumped onto him, and got into a full mount . . . ground and pound . . . I jumped on . . . and I was in a full mount and something came over me so instead of punching him I grabbed him by the neck and started choking him [imitates strangling motion], and I said, 'Come out of him devil! Come out of him devil!'"[28]

Bentley closes his talk by mentioning a Chinese man in need of healing who ended up with his tooth knocked out. "I called out this Chinese gentleman . . . and all of the sudden I went running down the

[26] "Todd Bentley Kicking People in the Face Revival," posted January 19, 2013, accessed February 3, 2017, https://youtu.be/OeAZ5IuydBA. This aired originally on GODTV during the Lakeland Revival in 2008. The text produced here has been transcribed from the video footage posted on YouTube.
[27] "Todd Bentley Kicking People in the Face Revival."
[28] Ibid.

aisle and I hit this guy so hard it drove him back several feet . . . he hit the ground, and his tooth popped right out of his mouth."[29]

Banned from the UK

Bentley was denied an entrance VISA to the UK in 2012 despite making his request according to the law. For all of Bentley's supposed healings in the loving name of Jesus Christ, Britain had seen similarly violent preachers, specifically, Smith Wigglesworth during the early 1900's. In a press release from the Home [immigration] Office, the following reasons were given:

> We can confirm that Mr. Bentley has been excluded from the UK. The government makes no apologies for refusing people access to the UK if we believe they are not conducive to the public good. Coming here is a privilege that we refuse to extend to those who might seek to undermine our society. [30]

Clearly the UK showed better judgment than the many followers and leaders like Bill Johnson who remain loyal to Todd Bentley. Since his affair, Bentley has gone from leading a revival of 400,000 people to small meetings across the US. Despite the decline in numbers, he continues to proclaim hundreds of thousands of salvations happening through his ministry and asks audiences to give their best offering.

Bill Johnson's lack of discernment in sharing his pulpit with men like Benny Hinn and Todd Bentley is a clear demonstration of his theology. These examples should serve as a sobering reminder that old heresies find a way to put on a new faces and re-emerge to separate people from their money, from healthy churches, and, ultimately, away from Jesus Christ.

Todd White and Gateway Church

The connections between Bill Johnson, Benny Hinn, and Todd Bentley, along with Jesus Culture and Bethel Music, should cause Christians to ask serious questions. Does modern evangelicalism need

---

[29] Ibid.

[30] Lizzy Davies, "Revivalist Preacher Todd Bentley Refused Entry to UK," *Guardian*, August 21, 2012, accessed February 3, 2017, https://www.theguardian .com/world/2012/aug/21/todd-bentley-refused-entry-to-uk.

to face the uncomfortable reality that we may lack discernment? Have we been turning a blind eye to Trojan horses infiltrating our ranks? Are we fearful of backlash if we stand up for truth? We must look in the mirror and ask ourselves these (and undoubtedly other) questions. The gospel of Jesus Christ and our witness for that gospel is on the line. Do we dare confuse the people of God by accepting without criticism these false teachers?

There is one final ministry that must be examined so that readers can understand how these groups interact and promote their false teachings. Popularity is no excuse for ignoring the truth, but this one may strike a nerve.

Gateway Church in Southlake, TX, is on the cutting edge of Third Wave culture. This megachurch boasts nearly 30,000 members including Dallas Cowboy players, famous celebrities, and of course, other influential ministry leaders. One of members of this church is Todd White, founder of Lifestyle Christianity. In 2017, Robert Morris, author of *The Blessed Life* and Senior Pastor of Gateway Church, allowed Todd White to preach during his, "Bring a Friend" series at Gateway Church.[31] In both 2016 and 2017, White has been a key speaker at the Jesus Conference which takes place in Orlando, FL, each year. In 2016 and 2017, this conference featured an all-star lineup of mystical-miracle workers such as Benny Hinn, Bill Johnson, Lou Engle, Daniel Kolenda, Michael Koulianos, Kenneth Copeland, and Reinhard Bonnke. It has become one of the top annual gatherings for these false prophets and teachers of corrupt doctrine. At the 2017 Jesus Conference, Benny Hinn laid hands on Todd White and gave him a special "word from the Lord."[32] He was also endorsed by Kenneth Copeland and has teamed up with him in an effort to raise $19 million for White's "Lifestyle Christianity Training Center" in Texas.[33] Robert Morris provided White with his own endorsement on the fundraising website.[34]

---

[31] "Todd Testimony–Bring a Friend Series," posted September 9, 2017, accessed October 15, 2017, https://youtu.be/f1Y1_FU8oA8.

[32] "Benny Hinn and Upper Room | Jesus '17," posted September 29, 2017, Jesus Image TV accessed October 15, 2017, https://youtu.be/mHAaVuZKBOo; begin at 4hr 20min.

[33] "Todd White & Kenneth Copeland – A Mandate to Multiply," posted November 2017, accessed December 26th, 2017, https://vimeo.com/241367590.

Gateway Church has produced recording artists such as Kari Jobe, long time worship leader who grew up under Robert Morris, while Bethel Church has produced the band Jesus Culture. Both embrace the same false doctrines espoused by their leaders. This isn't simply guilt by association—it's guilt by propagation of heretical theology found in Word of Faith and Prosperity Gospel teachings.

Evangelical leaders need to be on guard and aware of the dangers of false teaching. Our motivation for giving this information is not for sensationalism but to act as a warning. Jesus, as the Head of the church, has entrusted His bride to leaders who must regard themselves as servants, faithfully protecting His gospel.

When Sharing Isn't Caring

A seasoned Baptist pastor, who is a dear friend of mine [Anthony] and a Pentecostal pastor once took a missionary trip with me to China to deliver Bibles to churches who had a difficult time obtaining them. My Baptist pastor-friend shared thousands of Bibles. The Pentecostal shared his money to fund the project. They were ready to bless some desperate believers. The two men had very different views on certain doctrines that many would view as non-essential. The Pentecostal believed he possessed the gift of prophecy. The Baptist believed that the miraculous sign gifts were limited to the Apostolic era. The Pentecostal believed that a person could possess a private prayer language in another tongue, while the Baptist thought the idea of such a thing was silly. So how did they get along for ten days on a missionary trip? They agreed that none of their own versions of secondary doctrines would be taught on the trip, the Gospel would be delivered through standard Bibles, and they would preach only Jesus Christ's death and resurrection for believers. The Bibles were delivered legally, and the trip was a success. What's wrong with a partnership like this? Absolutely nothing. Neither man was a false teacher, neither taught their own doctrinal preferences or persuaded their recipients to speak in tongues. The taste of sweet biblical victory was experienced by both men as Bibles landed in the hands of believers who had never owned them before. That's some good old-fashioned missionary work that

---

[34] For a first-hand look at Todd White's $19 million project and major endorsers like Robert Morris, see www.lifestylechristianity.com.

shares resources, spreads the Gospel, and keeps the focus on Christ's salvific work on the cross.

So is there a point when cooperation between ministries (sharing) isn't caring? Can there be more harm than good done when certain partnerships are formed? To answer, let's reflect on the Apostle Paul's statement, "What then? Only that in every way, whether in pretense or in truth, Christ is proclaimed; and in this I rejoice, yes, and I will rejoice" (Phil 1:18). It's clear that Paul is saying that as long as a person is preaching the correct Christ (regardless of their sometimes questionable motives), we don't need to stop them or lose much sleep over them. But if it were that simple, the rest of this chapter wouldn't have been written. We need to pay close attention to what Paul wrote— *Christ* must be proclaimed. While Paul was in prison, these other preachers attempted to steal Paul's pulpit for personal gain. Yet the message they preached was still the true Gospel of Jesus Christ.

Both John and Paul were less gracious when it came to men and women who taught a false gospel. John was clear that the true believer should not associate with those who teach a false Gospel of Jesus Christ (2 John 9–11), while Paul exposed and accursed false teachers for their deception (2 Cor 11:13–15; Gal 1:8). Sharing isn't caring when we partner—for any purpose—with those who teach another gospel.

When it comes to deciding whom you should partner with, false teachers should never make the list. Paul campaigned against both the false doctrines and against the false teachers who had invaded the church at Corinth. He exhorted the church concerning the facts about the resurrection of Christ, commanded them not to be deceived, and then ordered them to steer clear of anyone who would corrupt their morality with lies about the Lord. It was within the context of false teaching that Paul wrote in 1 Corinthians 15:33–34, "Do not be deceived: 'Bad company corrupts good morals.' Become sober-minded as you ought, and stop sinning." Faithful preacher and theologian Warren Wiersbe commentates on Paul's words, writing:

> "Evil company corrupts good morals" is a quotation from the Greek poet Menander, a saying no doubt familiar to Paul's readers. The believer's body is the temple of God and must be kept separated from the sins of the world (2 Corinthians 6:14-7:1). To fellowship with the 'unfruitful works of darkness' (Ephesians

5:6-17) is only to corrupt God's temple. It was time for the Corinthians to *wake up* and *clean up*.[35]

Clearly it only takes a small drop of deception (like leaven) to compromise one's beliefs. Partnering with false teachers in exchange for an invitation to a major conference or offer of a favorable endorsement is never an acceptable transaction in God's eyes. Doctrinal disagreements over secondary issues like the method of water baptism or style of music are not reasons given in the Bible to reject fellowship with other Christians. However, when the discussion changes to false doctrines about Christ, his divine nature, his atonement on the cross and other essentials, it's healthy to draw strong lines of distinction. Partnering with false teachers so that you can reach their audience is a compromise that leads to corruption.

Simply put: avoid evil! When Paul established the church at Ephesus, his high conversion rate was bad for the false teaching business. Local idol makers had become rich, but their wealth was threatened by Paul's evangelism. As people turned to Christ, they no longer needed false idols. One idol-maker actually said, "our prosperity depends on this business" (Acts 19:25). Does this sound familiar? The idol-makers ran Paul out of town but not before the local church had been established. Later on, Paul provides a final warning to those remaining at Ephesus, "Be on guard for yourselves and for all the flock . . . I know that after my departure savage wolves will come in among you, not sparing the flock" (Acts 20:28-29).

There are many passages in Scripture that teach Christians to shun false teachers but perhaps none more clear than 2 Timothy 3:1-7. This passage describes the expected Christian response to the ravenous wolves taking advantage of desperate people and preying on the weak:

> But realize this, that in the last days difficult times will come. For men will be lovers of money, boastful, arrogant, revilers, disobedient to parents, ungrateful, unholy, unloving, irreconcilable, malicious gossips, without self-control, brutal, haters of good, treacherous, reckless, conceited, lovers of pleasure rather than lovers of God; holding to a form of godliness, although they have denied its power; and avoid such men as these. For among them are those

---

[35] Warren W. Wiersbe, *The Bible Exposition Commentary: New Testament*, 2nd ed. (Colorado Springs, CO: David C. Cook, 2008), 1:619

who enter households and captivate weak women weighed down with sins, led on by various impulses, always learning and never able to come to the knowledge of the truth. (2 Tim 3:1-7)

If there was ever any doubt that charlatan predators posing as representatives of Christ should be shunned and avoided, Paul's words should put that to rest. One way to detect a false teacher is to observe the fruit in their followers. Are the people being constantly taught but never growing in the knowledge of God or being sanctified by the power of the Holy Spirit through the Word? False teachers produce shallow disciples. As Paul described it, weak women were being swept up into the work of the false teachers, never experiencing a lasting and solid knowledge of the truth (2 Tim 3:6). It was obvious that these false teachers were simply dishing out empty doctrines that couldn't truly help anyone.

This is a highly personal topic for many Christians because it has direct implications on our familial relationships. In 2014, one family member and I [Costi] had a serious disagreement when I pleaded with them to stay away from Bethel's School of Supernatural Ministry. Another family member called me "full of hate" for trying to help them see that we had been living a lie, stating that "doctrine had ruined me." I'm not exactly welcome at many dinner tables during the holidays— though I don't seek out conflict on purpose. It just tends to happen when convictions clash over false teaching. That same year, we preached a series at our church entitled "Divergent." In this series we dealt with false religions and contrasted them with the truth of Scripture. Several people left the church after some of their favorite prosperity preachers were named. They called you "hateful" even though the sermons were sincerely temperate and lovingly preached— even through tears. This is what we must be willing to face if we're going to be faithful to the gospel. It's not always a war, but many times, it will cost you something to be a true disciple.

We ask, "What if a father, or brother, sister, or friend is a teacher who is preaching a false Gospel? Are you seriously telling me to avoid them altogether?" To answer these, we would remind you about this vital truth: every believer must proclaim the truth of God in love, and sometimes love demands we separate from those who can harm the church. Obedience to the Gospel of Jesus Christ will always be a dividing line between people. Christ declared:

Do not think that I came to bring peace on the earth; I did not come to bring peace, but a sword. For I came to set a man against his father, and a daughter against her mother, and a daughter-in-law; and a man's enemies will be the members of his own household. . . . And he who does not take his cross and follow after Me is not worthy of Me. (Matt 10:34–38)

For many Christians, Christ's words may or may not apply to immediate family, but if you ever fear ostracism, hatred, persecution, or rejection for standing up for truth, you would do well to count it a privilege to experience such suffering. Your reward for faithfulness awaits you in eternity: "For to you it has been granted for Christ's sake, not only to believe in Him, but also to suffer for His sake" (Phil 1:29).

Conclusion

In this chapter, we covered some of the heretical teachers Bill Johnson has chosen as his associates. While this provides clarity for Christians in regards to Johnson and Bethel Church, this case study points to a much broader truth in that birds of feather do flock together. Teachers such as these prove their lack of integrity by partnering together for personal gain and to preach a false gospel. Scripture clearly condemns this kind of partnership and we, as believers, must do whatever it takes to free ourselves from the shackles of divisive doctrine. Ultimately, the people of God must stand for truth regardless of the consequences. On this measure, let us mourn with A. W. Tozer who more than fifty years ago lamented:

The Church has surrendered her once lofty concept of God and has substituted for it one so low, so ignoble, as to be utterly unworthy of thinking, worshiping men. This she has not done deliberately, but little by little and without her knowledge; and her very unawareness only makes her situation all the more tragic.[36]

With so many clear warnings in Scripture, one begins to wonder, why so many well-intended young people are willing to accept as truth what the mystical-miracle movement teaches? The answer lies largely in the quirky ancestry we've documented in the previous chapters. Like a

---

[36] A. W. Tozer, *The Knowledge of the Holy: The Attributes Of God, Their Meaning In The Christian Life* (New York, NY: Harper & Row, 1961), 6.

master magician pulling from their box of tricks, each Sunday mystical-miracle teachers like Bill Johnson repackage the strategies of their Third Wave predecessors. In doing so, they continue in a long line of teachers who offer false hope and emotion as a cheap substitute for genuine spiritual transformation. In the next chapter, we'll try to overcome the emotional deception by using Johnson's doctrinal heresies as an illustration of their strategy.

5

Master Manipulation

Introduction

The best lies are those that contain a kernel of truth. The world's greatest manipulators attracted their audiences by offering a false product nearly indistinguishable from the real thing. Exactly, what are the stylings of a counterfeit teacher that make mystical-miracle teachers so influential? In this chapter we will examine some of the methods that Bill Johnson uses to beguile the starving sheep with his destructive doctrines. *Let us again be clear, these grievous errors do not belong to Johnson alone, we have simply selected Johnson for this case study due to his well-known purveyance of unbiblical teaching.*

Johnson is the premier mystical-miracle example. He is one of the most persuasive communicators who preys on the needs of his audience. The apostle Peter wrote in 2 Peter 2:1–3:

> But false prophets also arose among the people, just as there will also be false teachers among you, who will secretly introduce destructive heresies, even denying the Master who bought them, bringing swift destruction upon themselves. Many will follow their sensuality, and because of them the way of the truth will be maligned; and in *their* greed they will exploit you with false words; their judgment from long ago is not idle, and their destruction is not asleep.

False teachers are good communicators who understand how to manipulate feelings without directly addressing the need for individuals to pursue holiness. To do this they use highly stylized preaching and engaging music content that promises people immediate pleasure and prosperity—be it emotional or physical. This is a vital point: *if any teacher tells you the Gospel promises prosperity, power, or material reward, their message is not of God.*

Building a False Analogy

In logic, a false analogy is when a person connects two ideas with a common property and then wrongly creates a relationship to another property. For example, a man might say about his wife, "her smile lights up the room like the sun," but it would be wrong for someone to take this analogy to mean her mouth was filled with burning gasses that produce heat. While this example seems obvious, we need to apply this same discernment when interpreting the teachings of a teacher like Johnson.

One example of this false analogy arises in Johnson's book *When Heaven Invades Earth* (WHIE). In the opening to chapter 1, "The Normal Christian Life," Johnson boldly declares, "It is abnormal for a Christian not to have an appetite for the impossible."[1] At first, this sounds exciting, but what is the foundation for this claim? The fiction that Christians must pursue the impossible is loosely built, in our experience, from verses like Matthew 19:26 where Jesus says "with God, all things are possible." Coupled with James 4:2, "you lack only because you don't ask," manipulative teachers build a false analogy that Christians must always, in all things, have an appetite for impossible things.

However, there are serious questions that need to be asked when someone makes such an analogy: "Is this what either passage teaches?" "What is the definition of normal or abnormal?" "What impossible things did Jesus actually have in mind?" "Who determines the definition?" When any communicator begins with such a bold statement, intellectual honesty demands that the communicator clarify the definitions and tie it to clear biblical teaching rather than rely on false analogy. As we review the transcript from the sermon below, you will see that Johnson rarely backs his astounding claims with any objective truth. Instead, he allows each person's imagination to define the key words.

For example of this tactic let's examine one of Johnson's most well-known sermons. In this message, he shares with the Bethel

---

[1] Bill Johnson, *When Heaven Invades Earth: A Practical Guide To A Life Of Miracles* (Shippensburg, PA: Destiny Image, 2003), 25. The remainder of the book will often quote this work and will utilize the abbreviation WHIE for readability.

congregation his explanation of the signs and wonders taking place in their church, including falling gold dust and feathers. Johnson claims,

> We've been involved in this outpouring for fifteen years . . . really sixteen years now. And in this journey we've had the Lord show up and do a number of amazing things; one of the prominent things is the healing of bodies, deliverances from torment, restoration of families . . . all those kinds of things have been, uh, so extra-ordinary, so amazing.

> Occasionally we have unusual things happen. I don't take a service for . . . I just don't. I'll make reference and leave it alone. That's typically my response to the 'signs that make you wonder.' It was about fifteen, fourteen years ago probably, the feathers started appearing and falling in meetings . . . Then in our homes, then restaurants. You know. . . signs that make you wonder.

> People say, 'Where's that in your Bible?' Well, He [God] said 'He'd cover you with His feathers . . .' (laughter) 'Well, that's not literal,' they say. (laughter) And, that's what I thought . . . I thought it wasn't literal. It also says, 'there's healings in His wings . . .' Should make somebody happy. (laughter) Things like that happen. We'll have wind, gusts of wind I get hit with. Not imaginary things . . . you know. People get weird, I understand, they want something supernatural, so they imagine things. I understand that problem will always be with us. But, that is no reason to discount what He does do. We've had gold dust appear on people's hands for years. I don't ever talk about it . . . but frequently during worship, gold will fall. Today, I saw gold start falling during worship, this time during our prayer time. We'll just see it, drop like rain, I mean, you can't invite God into the house, and have something inside of your box happen! He's just slightly bigger than our understanding . . . yea . . . so these things happen with regularity. Sometimes they are things we go honestly for years and don't understand why [they come]) . . . but it happens at such a key moment, there's no way to question that it was the Lord.[2]

---

[2] Bill Johnson, "Response to Glory Cloud at Bethel," posted October 22, 2011, accessed December 15, 2016, https://youtu.be/tcPkOR4Lwj0.

Note the various false analogies presented in this sermon. Not only does each statement lack objective explanation, it rejects any argument that attempts to evaluate the mystic-miracle evidence in light of the Scripture. Johnson simply assumes as fact:

1. The Lord showed up to do these things.
2. These signs should make somebody happy.
3. If God is present, something "outside the box" must happen.
4. Gold and feathers indicates God being "slightly bigger" than our understanding.
5. The timing proves no one has the right to question the Lord.

Notice how Johnson builds multiple false analogies and discounts any critical analysis through a biblical filter. Look at these examples:

1. "That's not literal [in Bible]," people say. "That's what I thought . . ." [Johnson reasons].
2. "There's healing in His wings," the Bible means God wants to "make somebody happy".
3. Weird people will always be with us, but that's no reason to discount what God does.
4. We don't understand why signs come, but when they happen at key moment it must be God.

Do not miss the deception. In just four statements, Johnson has subtly argued to his congregation the following: (1) Your pastor doesn't take the Bible literally. (2) Signs should always make you happy. (3) We're normal and not weird. and, (4) Experience proves this is God. Just like a Jr. High student learning how to overcome the school bully, Johnson beats his opponents to the punch by answering their arguments before they're made by creating a false analogy between something true in Scripture and an emotional need in the hearer.

An Example of Johnson's Interpretative Method

Everyone with a love for God and His Word will immediately wonder, "What Bible verse is Johnson attempting to use for support?" Clearly, it is Psalm 91 where David writes, "He will cover you with His pinions (feathers) and under His wings you may seek refuge" (Psa 91:4). Hebrew scholars are not needed in order for us to recognize the obvious metaphorical value of David's words in this text. It's safe to assume that even a new Christian would discern David's descriptive poetry in these words and his use of analogy to express a powerful truth about God's love. The Bible is clear that God is spirit and does not have actual feathers or wings (John 4:24; cf. 1 Tim 6:16). Reading further through Psalm 91 supports the metaphoric nature of the text: God doesn't have a shadow (v. 1), and thus Johnson isn't really caught in a trapper's snare (v. 3), he isn't seeing arrows fly at him (v. 5), disease doesn't stalk people at night (v. 6), a thousand of Johnson's church members haven't died at his side (v. 7), nor does Johnson live in a tent (v. 10), angels aren't picking Johnson up in their hands (v. 12), and Johnson isn't walking on lions and cobras (v. 13). Clearly, the text is an expression of God's immense care for David and doesn't in any sense mean feathers literally fell on him. And most assuredly, this passage does not establish a normative expectation for the church.[3]

The ability to strip Scripture from its context and create these false analogies has inspired Johnson and many of his Third Wave/NAR adherents to use the Passion Translation of the Bible mentioned earlier in this book. Johnson has totally upended the epistemological cart: not only has he challenged the interpretation of Scripture as our sure source of knowledge, he has been instrumental in replacing the source of our knowledge with this new "translation." In an invaluable recent assessment of Johnson's biblical inaccuracy, professor Richard P. Moore points out how the NAR's recently released Passion Translation primes the pump for an entire new generation of decontextualized preaching.[4] Noted theologian Wayne Grudem implores all readers of the Scripture:

In a day when it is common for people to tell us how hard it is to

---

[3] This provides a good example of the importance of a proper hermeneutic. Only a consistently applied literal, grammatical-historical hermeneutic assures a reader from misapplying texts concerning Israel to the church and also ensures that each of Scripture's literary genres (e.g., prose or poetry) are interpreted according to their normal sense. For a solid work treating accurate biblical interpretation, see H. Wayne House and Forrest S. Weiland, eds., *The Theory and Practice of Biblical Hermeneutics: Essays in Honor of Elliot E Johnson* (Silverton, OR: Lampion Press, 2015).

[4] Richard P. Moore, *Divergent Theology: An Inquiry Into the Theological Characteristics of the Word of Faith Third Wave Movement and The New Apostolic Reformation* (CreateSpace, 2017), 96–97.

interpret Scripture rightly, we would do well to remember that not once in the Gospels do we ever hear Jesus saying anything like this: "I see how your problem arose—the Scriptures are not very clear on that subject." Instead, whether he is speaking to scholars or untrained common people, his responses always assume that the blame for misunderstanding any teaching of Scripture is not to be placed on the Scriptures themselves, but *on those who misunderstand* or fail to accept what is written."[5] [emphasis mine]

Friends, the words of the Bible are God's words. We are not allowed to insert our own theological opinions to advance a movement or prop up false teachers. What we see taking place here is the willingness of Johnson to call into question the clarity of the Bible, place personal experience above God's revealed Word, and, ironically, make God unknowable without Johnson's mystic reinterpretation. In essence, he's just looked his church in the eye and said, "I can say *whatever* I want about the Bible, and you need to trust me." Towards the end of the clip we see the classic egotism of a false teacher as Johnson speaks with a smirk, "I thought it was literal [too]. . . ." This unauthentic remark reveals Johnson's heart, that he believes he has a special in with God (or a god) and is receiving truth not available to the rest of Christianity.

An Example of Bill Johnson's Monopolization

The advent of technology and social media means that Johnson's manipulation of truth is coming to a church near you. This technological platform has provided him with a far greater ability to influence the next generation than many of his Third Wave predecessors. From the arts to leadership training, Bethel Church's ministry ecosystem is fueled by a steady diet of teaching that comes directly from Johnson's manipulative pulpit. We will review a few of these corruptions below.

Bethel Supernatural School of Ministry
The Bethel Supernatural School of Ministry (BSSM) promises the impartation of signs and wonders, supernatural power, and revival training for anyone 18 and over. This school is unaccredited, yet boasts

---

[5] Wayne Grudem, *Systematic Theology*, 106.

two thousand students paying upwards of $10,000 to complete the program.[6] Students are unaware of the deception they've fallen victim to until years later. We've spent hours in counseling sessions with students who have been confused and spiritually abused by BSSM and other affiliated revivalist training schools.

BSSM students have certainly made headlines for their grave suck-ing necromancy (which we'll address in the next chapter). But what makes BSSM so dangerous is that it has produced countless alumni who are leading children and churches into darkness under the guise of light. One of the most notable leaders is Seth Dahl, Children's Pastor at Bethel Church. The curriculum he employs is another spin off of Bethel's approach to Christianity.[7] Under his direction, children are taught to take imaginary trips to Heaven, visit with imaginary angels, and hold their own miracle healing services while their parents sit under Johnson's teaching in the sanctuary.

WorshipU

Bethel Music and their band Jesus Culture have helped Johnson reach a global audience. It seems only fitting then that they offer a form of training to further influence and capitalize on the Christian music industry.[8] In keeping with the theme of "Heaven invading earth," Bethel's Worship University offers instruction from Brian Johnson, Jenn Johnson, Bill Johnson and many others, training musicians on how to cultivate Bethel's version of a "lifestyle of worship." A steady stream of popular musicians is helpful to the success of any millennial ministry, and Bethel Church promotes and utilizes their music division more than any of the other mystical-miracle ministries.

Bethel Conservatory of the Arts

Johnson calls his Conservatory of the Arts the "fulfillment of a di-vine assignment."[9] Launched in Fall 2017, the Bethel Conservatory of

---

[6] Bethel School of Supernatural Ministry, accessed December 8, 2017, http://bssm.net/.

[7] A child's psychological development is very malleable in the early years of their life. See, "Child Development," Wikipedia, accessed February 22, 2017, https://en.wikipedia.org/wiki/Child_development.

[8] WorshipU, accessed December 8, 2017, https://worshipu.com/.

[9] Bethel Conservatory of the Arts, accessed December 8, 2017, https://www

the Arts seeks to impact the art world through acting and drama in ways that align with Bethel's mission to bring the kingdom to the nations.

Bethel Christian School

Beyond the local church and post-secondary schools, Bethel has operated an elementary school since 1988.[10] Kindergarten through 8th graders are inundated with a fully loaded "supernatural" curriculum.[11] A phone call to Bethel Christian School in April 2017 revealed that they consider themselves more of a ministry of Bethel Church, but comply with all California State standards and are ACSI accredited. When we asked if the school's teaching was theologically consistent with the Sunday teaching of Seth Dahl and Bill Johnson, the reply was, "Yes, the children will receive consistent teaching if they're in Sunday school and in the classroom with us all week."

Global Legacy's Leadership Training

Finally, Bethel's Global Legacy Leadership Training (GL) will sell anyone the ability to activate encounters with God, become an apostle, make others an apostle, and "breakthrough" (a term left undefined). Packages range from $59–$875, depending if one's desire is to be empowered or be turned into an apostle.[12] These distance-learning programs spread Johnson's theology and promise to make people apostles in exchange for money. This practice is justified nowhere in Scripture nor is there any biblical foundation for the belief that the apostolic gift, given by the Holy Spirit alone, can be purchased through an online training program. The most dangerous aspect of this network's influence is on those who join the Global Legacy: Iris Global (Heidi Baker), Bethel Prophetic, and the Healthcare Network where they promise to "manifest the healing power of Jesus."[13] The goal of the medical connection is:

.bethelconservatory.com/.

[10] Bethel Christian School, accessed July 19, 2017, http://bcsredding.org/.

[11] Bethel Christian School, accessed July 19, 2017, http://bcsredding.org/about-us/#who-we-are. The BCS website clearly specifies that they teach the children that "signs and wonders follow those who believe."

[12] "Training," Global Legacy, accessed December 8, 2017, http://www.globallegacy.com/training.

[13] "About," Healthcare Network, accessed December 8, 2017, http://health

Cohorts of healthy patients; waiting times reduced due to supernatural healing; unexpected remission of cancer; accessible healthcare for all; pioneering surgical techniques; research and development of new medications; a legacy of top level trainees; surgeries without scars; peer-reviewed case reports of the miraculous; administrative excellence; innovative, proven uses for natural remedies; medical professionals who are themselves healed - body, soul and spirit - and work from a place of identity derived in Christ, not their title. . . .[14]

This appears to be a modern-day innovation of faith-healers like Wigglesworth with the medical aspirations of Oral Robert's center for medicine.

Conclusion

In this chapter we have expanded on the deceptive logic used by Johnson to strip the Scripture of its context. This allows him and other mystical-miracle teachers to manipulate the emotions of their followers and build trust in their self-claimed apostolic authority for interpreting God's Word. We also outlined some of the ministries in the arts, education, and medicine Johnson uses to expand his influence. We do not write these words with joy, but with a heavy heart for the next generation of believers. Out of love for our children and for our brothers and sisters lost in deception, we believe these facts demand that evangelicals unite in calling Bethel Church and the mystical-miracle movement to repentance. Johnson's manipulative methodology is based, ultimately, in heretical theology which we'll now analyze in the next chapter.

---

care.globallegacy.com/.
[14] "About," Healthcare Network.

6

Doctrinal Deception

Introduction

There is a wise saying, "Put your feet in the right place before you stand." Even the most beautiful building if erected on a compromised foundation will soon collapse, Jesus observed in Matthew 7:24-27. In this chapter we examine four theologies undergirding the music and ministry of the mystical-miracle movement, using Bethel Church and Bill Johnson as our ongoing illustration.

One of my [Anthony] favorite Sunday school songs growing up was about a wise man who built his house on the rock and a foolish man who built his house upon the sand. The passage is from Jesus' teaching in Matthew 7 (mentioned above). If you grew up singing the song, you remember the best part came at the end after the rains fell and the foolish man's house fell down. Every kid—if you had the cool teacher—was allowed to fall on the floor, simulating the collapse of the house. As a child it seemed like innocent fun. But now, as a pastor who has seen the effect of theological instability on people's lives, the reality behind the song is chilling. Far too many people have built their entire life on shifting sand. The mystical-miracle movement has built their entire belief system on a bad foundation. Everything we've discussed so far, including the heretical heritage and the manipulation of congregations and followers—all rests on a corrupt foundation of unbiblical theology.

Bill Johnson's basic beliefs were originally documented in his 2003 book, *When Heaven Invades Earth* (WHIE). We reviewed the content of WHIE and compared it with material from two of Johnson's later books, *Releasing the Spirit of Prophecy* (RSP) and *Supernatural Power of a Transformed Mind* (SPTM), to discern if there were developments or adjustments in his theology over the intervening years.[1]

While it did not take long to survey the books, it did take considerable time to isolate the staggering amount of misinformation contained in each volume. By far, the most difficult part of our analysis was trying to determine the method of biblical interpretation behind Johnson's Kingdom Now theology.[2] Each book appears to be the accumulation of disconnected Bible verses, strung together to give his theology some degree of biblical authority.

Based on the sheer volume of troubling material, we've chosen to highlight and address only the repetitive statements in his books. There are many important points we could address, but we chose to focus on the error of those views which Johnson himself finds significant. As you read this chapter, we implore you to consider these basic questions—Should a man be allowed to pastor God's flock if he: (1) Teaches a wrong view of Jesus? (2) Impugns the faith of suffering saints? (3) Persistently misinterprets Scripture? (4) Reconstructs the economy of the Trinity? (5) Pronounces unfulfilled prophecy? or (6) Contends

---

[1] Bill Johnson, *When Heaven Invades Earth: A Practical Guide to a Life of Miracles*; *Releasing the Spirit of Prophecy: The Supernatural Power of Testimony* (Shippensburg, PA: Destiny Image, 2014); and *The Supernatural Power of a Transformed Mind: Access to a Life of Miracles* (Shippensburg, PA: Destiny Image, 2005).

[2] Dominion (Kingdom Now) theology advocates generally trace their view to Genesis 1:28 where many have recognized a "dominion mandate" given to Adam and Eve, viz., to have dominion over God's creation as His representatives. Twisting this out of context, some promote aberrant versions suggesting Satan, not God, has full dominion over the earth and that man's responsibility is to regain that dominion. While Bill Johnson's exact position regarding dominion theology is admittedly difficult to define, he has made statements that suggest a distorted dominionism. For example, Johnson has publicly taught that "We make a mistake in thinking [God] is control of everything . . . He comes at our invitation because He has released the dominion to us." In the same message, Johnson goes on to state: "If you believe God is in control of everything then you have to look at Christ as some tragedy and say He allowed it for some purpose." "Bill Johnson - Word Faith-Dominion Now," September 3, 2010, accessed January 31, 2018, https://youtu.be/EhG1x4fOtBw. Remarkably, Johnson's statements run in stark contrast to Peter who preached that Christ's death was indeed a part of God's predetermined plan and foreknowledge (Acts 2:23). Contrary to Johnson's views, God is not so limited in power that He must act at our invitation, and further, nothing is outside of God's rule, control, and/or dominion.

Jesus won't return until all sickness is healed?

Doctrinal Error #1 "You and I Are the Same as Jesus"

From the perspective of Christian orthodoxy, the most pernicious error in Johnson's theology is the confusion surrounding the person of Jesus. Specifically, Johnson's teaching that confuses the nature of Jesus with the nature of man. Our clearest understanding of Jesus is, of course, found in the Scripture. Yet, the person of Christ is also well captured in the historic Apostles Creed:

> We believe in God, the Father almighty, creator of heaven and earth.

> We believe in Jesus Christ, his only Son, our Lord, who was conceived by the Holy Spirit and born of the virgin Mary. He suffered under Pontius Pilate, was crucified, died, and was buried; he descended to hell. The third day he rose again from the dead. He ascended to heaven and is seated at the right hand of God the Father almighty. From there he will come to judge the living and the dead.

> We believe in the Holy Spirit, the holy universal church, the communion of saints, the forgiveness of sins, the resurrection of the body, and the life everlasting. Amen.

But in a clear rejection of Jesus' divine nature, Johnson begins the second chapter of *When Heaven Invades Earth* with this outrageous statement: "He (Jesus) performed *miracles, wonders, and signs*, as a man in right relationship to God . . . not as God. If He performed miracles because He was God, then they would be unattainable for us."[3] Johnson's theology traces its roots to the English preacher Edward Irving (1792–1834). Considered the first reformed Pentecostal, Irving taught that we live our life as an analogy to the life of Christ. This teaching emphasized, "that Christ in nature was made the same as Man and thus we can be made like Him through the power of the Holy Spirit."[4] Irving's Christology was later declared heretical by the Church of Scotland, and Johnson's teaching should be considered no less divisive.

---

[3] Johnson, *When Heaven Invades Earth*, 29.
[4] Miller, *Promise of the Father*, 9.

Further in the book, Johnson explains that "the name Jesus Christ implies that Jesus is the one smeared [or anointed] with the Holy Spirit."[5] Misusing the term "Christ" (Greek, *Christos*) to mean that Jesus had no power to minister except that he was anointed by the Holy Spirit. Johnson goes on to repeatedly state that Jesus "laid His divinity aside" to simply live as a man in right relationship to God.[6] Johnson's words harken back to the days of Irving who wrote, "all the works of Christ were done by the man who anointed with the Holy Ghost, and not by the God mixing himself up with the man."[7]

Historically, this form of theology, called *kenotic* theology, has been challenged by the church because it deemphasizes the deity of Christ and unbalances the hypostatic union of Christ being the one hundred percent God-man.[8] Kenotic theology dates back to the German philosophers of the 19th century, most of whom followed Hegel (the philosophical forerunner of communism and fascism) in their attempt to explain that Philippians 2:7 describes Christ "emptying himself" of divine attributes. Noted theologian Wayne Grudem refutes this interpretation:

> No recognized teacher in the first 1,800 years of church history, including those who were native speakers of Greek, thought that "emptied himself" in Philippians 2:7 meant the Son of God gave up some of his divine attributes. Second, . . . the text does not say that Christ "emptied himself of some powers". . . . Third, the text *does* describe what Jesus did by "emptying": he did not do it by giving up any of his attributes but rather by "taking the form of a servant," that is, by coming to live as a man. . . . The context interprets the "emptying" as equivalent to "humbling himself." [9]

---

[5] Johnson, *When Heaven Invades Earth*, 79.

[6] Ibid., 79, 87–88.

[7] Edward Irving, "Facts Connected with Recent Manifestations of Spiritual Gifts," *Fraser's Magazine* (January, March, April 1832): 757, quoted in C. Gordon Strachan, *The Pentecostal Theology of Edward Irving* (Peabody, MA: Hendrickson, 1973), 65.

[8] Stephen M. Smith, "Kenosis, Kenotic Theology," in *Evangelical Dictionary of Theology*, ed. Walter A. Elwell, 2nd ed. (Grand Rapids, MI: Baker, 2001), 651; and, Paul Enns, *The Moody Handbook of Theology*, rev. ed. (Chicago, IL: Moody Publishers, 2014), 242, 751.

[9] Wayne Grudem, *Systematic Theology*, 550.

Smith admits that "All forms of classical orthodoxy explicitly reject principle kenotic theology."[10] Louis Berkhof expands upon this error:

The theory is based on the pantheistic conception that God and man are not so absolutely different but that the one can be transformed into the other. The Hegelian idea of *becoming* is applied to God, and the absolute line of demarcation is obliterated.[11]

Johnson continues to parrot this Christological error in his book *The Supernatural Power of a Transformed Mind*, writing:

Jesus had no ability to heal the sick. He couldn't cast out devils, and He had no ability to raise the dead. He said of Himself in John 5:19, "the Son can do nothing of Himself." He had set aside His divinity . . . He put self-imposed restrictions on Himself to show us that we could do it, too. Jesus so emptied Himself that He was incapable of doing what was required of Him by the Father—without the Father's help.[12]

Bill Johnson is preaching the same heresy we see taught by the likes of Edward Irving and condemned by the church throughout history. He is preaching a Jesus different from the Jesus revealed in the Scripture and affirmed by historic Christian councils. For one hundred years, between A.D. 350–450, at least three significant heretical positions pertaining to Christ arose demanding church response. One position was that of Apollinarius who stressed the deity of Christ but discredited the bodily nature of Christ. The council of Constantinople quickly silenced this teaching. A second illegitimate position was that of Eutyches who taught a blending of Jesus' two natures into a third separate mixture of the two. The doctrine of redemption was in danger so an imperial council reeducated Eutyches.

However, the fundamental heresy that defined early 4th century theology and most of our orthodox foundation was that of Arius, an influential pastor of the Baucalis Church, who asserted that Jesus had a human nature but that His deified nature was not wholly God. In one

---

[10] Smith, "Kenosis, Kenotic Theology," 651. Despite this statement, Smith endorses kenotic theology.

[11] Louis Berkhof, *Systematic Theology* (Grand Rapids, MI: Eerdmans, 1965), 328.

[12] Johnson, *Supernatural Power of a Transformed Mind*, 50.

sense Arius taught Jesus was a lesser being, a first created being, half-god, and not entirely God. This teaching appealed to influential groups such as the Gnostics (much like it does for today's Mormons and Jehovah Witnesses), because it rejected Christ's dual natures (God/man) as well as him being the *only* way, truth, and life. However, in A.D. 325, Constantine recognized the explosive nature of the issue and called a council of 300 pastors to meet at Nicaea. The debate raged for many years as the council attempted to determine if Jesus was *homoiousios* "similar" to God or whether He was *homoousios* the "same" as God.[13] In the end, the followers of Arius were condemned as heretics because their theology of Christ as less than fully God degenerated Christianity into a form of mere paganism.[14] Church leaders knew that if people accepted the teaching of Arius, the faith would be left with two gods, Jesus would be declared neither god nor man, God the Father would remain unapproachable, and Jesus the Son could offer mankind no hope. The Council of Nicaea proved the importance of each word in Holy Scripture and that Jesus was 100% God-man—two distinct and unmixed natures in one person.

Johnson, through Pentecostal forerunners like Irving, has taken the Arian position. Johnson's purpose in taking this doctrinal position is clear throughout WHIE as he attempts to encourage Christians to operate in the same status and giftedness of Christ. He continually uses broad brushstrokes, such as, "We are God's workmanship" and "Jesus told His disciples they'd do greater works than these"—to paint a picture of methodological equality with Christ.

In SPTM Johnson states, "We have the right to become like Christ, our Elder Brother . . . We are destined to be fully restored to the image and likeness of God. . . ."[15] Johnson's term elder brother is strikingly similar to the Jehovah Witness teaching that wrongly interprets the word "firstborn" in Colossians 1:15 to mean "first created," making Jesus out as a created being. A proper interpretation

---

[13] See, G. W. Bromiley, "Christology" in *The International Standard Bible Encyclopedia*, ed. by Geoffrey W. Bromiley, rev. ed. (Grand Rapids, MI: Eerdmans, 1979-1988), 663-664.

[14] F. J. Foakes-Jackson, "Arianism," in *Encyclopedia of Religion and Ethics*, ed. James Hastings, John A. Selbie, and Louis H. Gray (New York: Charles Scribner's Sons, 1908-1926), 777.

[15] Johnson, *Supernatural Power of a Transformed Mind*, 31.

of Colossians 1:15 makes "first-born" related to the transferable title of preeminence used elsewhere in Scripture (Gen 41:51–52; Jer 31:9). The Scriptures do not teach that we are the same as Jesus. Or more clearly, they do not teach that Jesus was born like us. Each New Testament writer was clear to describe himself as a bond slave of the sinless Messiah Jesus. Johnson's teaching follows the age-old quest desiring the deification of man; a heretical quality common to Johnson's ancestry of word-faith teachers like Kenneth Copeland, Benny Hinn, and many more.

What does it really mean for a Christian to receive the new nature or new heart? When the believer is born again by the work of Jesus through the power of the Holy Spirit, we enter into the family of God. Our old nature is defeated, crucified with Christ, and we receive a new nature that desires the things of God (Rom 6:13; 2 Cor 5:17). To be born again means that we are recreated as new people with a new nature of righteousness and holiness (Eph 4:24) that desires the same things that Christ desires. This has nothing to do with works of wonder. In essence, believers love what Christ loves and hate what Christ hates (1 John 4:4), believers have the power to conquer temptation (1 Cor 10:13), and are slowly conformed to the image of Christ (2 Cor 6:18) until the time of death when their soul is taken to Heaven and they are perfected (Heb 12:23). Again, this has nothing to do with performing miracles like Jesus.

Amazingly, for all of Johnson's discussion about Christ's power, there is no clear Gospel message in *When Heaven Invades Earth*. Despite its title, there is no mention of man's sin and Christ's atonement until a third of the way through when Johnson writes, "God confronts sin, forgiveness is given."[16] The book contains no mention of God's wrath or man's necessary repentance. Further, the mention of atonement is immediately cloaked in more pithy health and wellness speech: "when His rule collides with disease, people are healed."[17] This theme continues throughout the book, as healing after healing is described with no clarity as to how the supposed healing leads to Gospel understanding and eternal transformation.

In this fundamental Christological error, Johnson has displayed two characteristics of a false teacher—distorting the person of Jesus and

---

[16] Johnson, *When Heaven Invades Earth*, 62.
[17] Ibid., 62.

willingly teaching recognized heretical doctrines. Johnson's confusion surrounding basic Christology alone disqualifies him as a Gospel minister and demands that he repent. In the next section we'll see how Johnson uses this Christological error as a to platform for the second flawed message.

Doctrinal Error #2: Sick People Just Need More Faith

Early in WHIE Johnson tells the story of a miracle wedding where a man is supposedly healed in the kitchen while the bride and groom looked on. After describing the scene, he makes the statement, "There wasn't a great person involved, except for Jesus. All the rest of us simply made room for God, believing Him to be good 100 percent of the time. . . . In the midst of this marriage celebration God invaded a home marked by hellish disease"[18] So what is the importance of this story in Johnson's theology?

Relying on his heretical theology of Jesus as his foundational hermeneutic, Johnson builds his second errant doctrine on a misapplication of Matthew 16. In this commission from Jesus to his disciples, Johnson reads into the text the promise that believers have authority to wield and perform miracles on earth. Jesus says, "I will give you the keys of the kingdom of heaven; and whatever you shall bind on earth shall have been bound in heaven and whatever you loose on earth shall have been loosed in heaven" (Matt 16:19).

Johnson uses this verse as justification for his healing power at the miracle wedding and subsequently teaches that all Christians should be wielding power just as Jesus did. Again, make sure you're reading this clearly: Bill Johnson contends that because Jesus was just like us (error #1) and relied on the Holy Spirit for his power, all Christians can expect to wield the healing power like Jesus. The key failure of Johnson's teaching is to recognize the context of Matthew 16. Jesus in no way suggests that his authority, or the power he was passing on, was the ability to do signs and wonders. In fact, the "keys of the kingdom" represent the authority to preach the Gospel of Christ (v. 19) and thus to open the door of Heaven. As Unger observed, the keys of the kingdom were given by Jesus to his apostles so that they could unlock the power of God's grace: from Jerusalem, to Judea, to Samaria and to

---

[18] Johnson, *When Heaven Invades Earth*, 27.

the uttermost parts of the world.[19] The purpose of Jesus' words in Matthew 16 is not to grant mystical-miracle power to his disciples, but to establish himself as the Messiah who unlocks the power of God's promised salvation to all the world.

So if, as Johnson claims, every Christian has the power to heal, then why are so many sick? The failure to be healed, concludes Johnson, must then be the lack of faith . . . it's your fault you are sick. The concept that sick people need more faith[20] is a theme for Johnson who believes that "sickness is to the body what sin is to the soul."[21] According to Johnson, sickness comes from lack of faith or demonic forces. As you may imagine, this is an oft-used statement found in all Third Wave/NAR theology because it provides not only a justification for their failed healings but also a clear-cut enemy to be overcome.

Does the Bible attribute sickness to a lack of faith or to hellish interference? The answer is clearly no. In fact, the Bible teaches that even though sickness came into the world as a result of Adam and Eve's rebellion, God is still sovereign over his creation (Ex 4:11). In Johnson's view, the power of God is limited by our faith and thwarted by the devil. He promotes a God who is weak without your cooperation, while the portrait painted by the Bible is of a God who is still in charge of His creation. Sometimes God heals based on prayer and His good will. At other times, His plan includes illness and death, allowing true saints to shine amidst earth's darkest circumstances.

As one would assume, Johnson's false teaching on health blends well with His promise of riches and prosperity: "Is anyone starving in heaven? Of course not! This request is a practical application of how His dominion should be seen here on earth—abundant supply."[22] Friends, it is an egotistical, first-world American, driving an Aston Martin who would dare say such an ignorant and insensitive thing. How do you tell Christian brothers starving in Kenya or enduring

---

[19] See, Frederick Merrill Unger, "The Baptism with the Holy Spirit Part 3," *Bibliotheca Sacra* 101, no. 404 (October 1944): 486–88. Of importance is to see this passage in Matthew as a fulfillment of prophecy given in Isaiah 22:22. The authority is given by Jesus because he is the promised Messiah. Cf. Hans Wildberger, *Isaiah 13–27*, A Continental Commentary (Minneapolis, MN: Fortress Press, 1997), 402.

[20] Johnson, *When Heaven Invades Earth*, 45, 53, 75.

[21] Ibid., 45.

[22] Ibid., 60.

martyrdom in the Middle East that they simply "don't have enough faith" in the Kingdom or else it would arrive in material abundance? Their *daily* faith in suffering trial upon trial is built on a greater Kingdom to come, precisely as the apostle Paul promised (2 Cor 4:17). For thousands of years, from slaves to paupers, it has been faith in the *coming* kingdom that brought hope and enduring faith in the midst of pain.

In a more recent work, Johnson attempts to respond to these questions after acknowledging failed healings in his own church and the death of his own father. Johnson admits:

> We had to make a choice regarding what we were going to believe about God in the face of this *contradiction*. We had to come back to the truth that the problem was still on our end. The problem is never on God's end. He is good, and He hasn't changed . . . For clarification, when I say the problem is on our end, it doesn't imply that God was disappointed with us or somehow at odds with us. It doesn't imply that we had misheard what God had said, were being disobedient, or that what we did was entirely ineffective. It just means that the problem is part of the reality of living in a world that still does not express the will of God on earth.[23]

Johnson's admission epitomizes the faith dilemma for all who claim health and wealth. The empirical data all rests in direct contradiction of their fundamental claim. There are faithful people who get sick and wicked people who remain well. If any man purports to be a healer he must examine why his efforts have failed—either he is faithless or his theology of sin and suffering is flawed. We are writing to give hope to everyone suffering under the guilt of Third Wave/NAR theology. You are not a victim. Your faith is not flawed. You have simply been sold a false theology by false teachers.

The primary difference between the healing Johnson teaches and the healing ministry of Jesus is that Jesus had a 100% success rate. A study of the Gospels reveal that Jesus healed when and how he chose, not based on the faith of people. In many cases, he healed despite the lack of faith (Matt 8:5-13; Mark 1:23-26; 9:17-29, Luke 17:11-19, John 5:1-16), making Christ's miracle ministry different from anything

---

[23] Johnson, *Releasing the Spirit of Prophecy*, 127.

promoted by Johnson. Johnson's quote above makes it clear he takes no responsibility for his failed healings, but praise God we serve a Jesus who never failed.

The fatal doctrinal flaw in Johnson's teaching on healing occurs when he reasons that the death of Christ is a guarantee that people will be healed in this life of every physical malady. He teaches his congregation:

> No, two thousand years ago Jesus made a purchase. He does not decide not to heal people today. The decision two thousand years ago was to heal. Either the payment was sufficient for all sin or no sin. Either the payment was sufficient for all sickness or no sickness... The brushstrokes of God's redemption was to wipe out the root of sin, the root of illness and the root of poverty."[24]

As we mentioned before, every effective lie is mixed with some truth. The lie in Johnson's theology is that that Christ's atoning death was meant to make people healthy and wealthy in this life. What is the truth? Yes, there is a promise of full-healing in the atonement of Christ. Everyone who is saved by Christ will be fully freed from sin and from sickness and from poverty, but that will not be fulfilled until Christ returns. Fourteen centuries ago, Aurelius Augustine, Bishop of Hippo shared this story of a woman healed of breast cancer:

> In the same city of Carthage lived Innocentia, a very devout woman of the highest rank in the state. She had cancer in one of her breasts, a disease which, as physicians say, is incurable. Ordinarily, therefore, they either amputate, and so separate from the body the member on which the disease has seized, or, that the patient's life may be prolonged a little, though death is inevitable even if somewhat delayed, they abandon all remedies, following, as they say, the advice of Hippocrates. This the lady we speak of had been advised to by a skillful physician, who was intimate with her family; and she betook herself to God alone by prayer. On the approach of Easter, she was instructed in a dream to wait for the first woman that came out from the baptistery after being baptized, and to ask her to make the sign of Christ upon her sore.

---

[24] Bill Johnson, "Does God Ever Cause Sickness?" posted October 26, 2009, accessed April 20, 2016, https://youtu.be/0iXrX9eSHWA.

She did so, and was immediately cured. The physician who had advised her to apply no remedy if she wished to live a little longer, when he had examined her after this, and found that she who, on his former examination, was afflicted with that disease was now perfectly cured, eagerly asked her what remedy she had used, anxious, as we may well believe, to discover the drug which should defeat the decision of Hippocrates. But when she told him what had happened, he is said to have replied, with religious politeness, though with a contemptuous tone, and an expression which made her fear he would utter some blasphemy against Christ, "I thought you would make some great discovery to me." She, shuddering at his indifference, quickly replied, *"What great thing was it for Christ to heal a cancer, who raised one who had been four days dead?"*[25]

There, absolutely, is healing in the cross. It is not based on our faith (or lack of faith). It is not based on works. It is not based on merit. It is based on the shed blood of Jesus. But in this life, we still suffer because of the sin of the world in hopes that more people may be reached with the power of the Gospel. Every one of us will end this life in death. Every faith-healer gets sick. Every faith-healer will die. Their faith can't do anything to change that. But when this life has passed, we will all move on to eternity where death will be finally crushed and we will live in total health and true Kingdom prosperity (greater than any riches promised by today's charlatans).

But in debunking these first two Gospel errors, we must move on because Johnson is not done. In the next section we'll look at a false hope in Johnson's utopia for today.

Doctrinal Error #3: The Kingdom of Heaven is Now

A third corrupt doctrine from Johnson is that Bethel Church will lead the earth in a one billion-person miracle revival, ushering in a kingdom state of perfection, paving the way for Christ's return.[26] In theolog-

---

[25] Augustine of Hippo, "The City of God," in *St. Augustin's City of God and Christian Doctrine*, ed. Philip Schaff, trans. Marcus Dods, vol. 2, A Select Library of the Nicene and Post-Nicene Fathers of the Christian Church, First Series (Buffalo, NY: Christian Literature Company, 1887), 486–487; emphasis added.

[26] Johnson, *When Heaven Invades Earth*, 182. Astute theology students will recognize this as having its roots in postmillennial eschatology. A word should

ical circles this is called Kingdom Now theology and presupposes that it is man's job to fix earth so that Jesus can return. In order to promote his Kingdom Now theology, Johnson once again distorts the plain reading of Scripture. The foundation for his abuse is in interpreting Genesis 1 as a time when Satan took control of earth and man was given the job of defeating darkness. Johnson concludes, "the Father wanted Satan defeated by man.[27]

Johnson's subversive theology is not new. The Kingdom Now theology was nascent in early Pentecostalism and gained traction in early 20th century liberalism when people believed the world would be evangelized, grow more peaceful, and usher in the Kingdom. William Newton Clarke, a noted pundit of this liberal social-gospel, stated, "If our Lord will but complete the spiritual coming that he has begun, there will be no need of a visible advent to make perfect his glory on the earth."[28] The overarching theme of this movement was that humanity would increasingly improve as Christians fixed things for God and establish his kingdom now, on earth.

This theology gave rise to theories of special sonship associated with the Latter Rain movement. The New Order of the Latter Rain dates back to 1948 and was influenced by Franklin Hall and William Branham (discussed earlier in this book). In his 1946 work, *Atomic Power With God*, Hall writes, "Satan was not too much interested in the Christ until He was ready to MANIFEST his sonship."[29] This statement sparks a question: What did it look like when Jesus suddenly manifested his sonship? Hall continues:

After Jesus received the Holy Spirit, although He was the Son of God yet [sic] He did not begin to manifest His Sonship until after

---

also be said distinguishing the Kingdom Now or Dominion theology of Pentecostalism from that of the Dominionism or Christian Reconstructionism of Covenantal-Reformed branches of theology. While both are rooted in postmillennialism, their versions of dominionism manifest differently.

[27] Ibid., 30-32. Johnson expands on this in *Supernatural Power of a Transformed Mind*, 30-51.

[28] William Newton Clark, *An Outline of Christian Theology* (New York: Scribner, 1901), 444.

[29] Franklin Hall, *Atomic Power With God: Through Prayer and Fasting* (San Diego, CA: Franklin Hall, 1946), chap. 4, accessed December 19, 2017, http://standsure.net/books/hall.htm.

He had fasted forty days. As children of God we will need to follow Jesus in fasting and prayer, if we expect to manifest spiritual life and power, as did our Lord. There is no other way to have a full manifestation of spirituality but through fasting and prayer, and there is, according to St. Paul, no other remedy for the groaning and suffering of creation than a complete manifestation of the children of God, as far as is possible here on earth. Rom. 8:19-22: "The whole creation groaneth and travaileth in pain together until now, and waiteth for the manifestation of the sons of God, for the creature was made subject to vanity. [30]

These statements spark another vital question: What does it mean that we, like Jesus, are also to manifest sonship? We can see as early as 1946 that distinctions between Jesus and the believer were being blurred. Romans 8:19-22 became the key proof text that Latter Rain/Third Wave/NAR would come to rely upon in their mission to raise up an army-like end times generation. Their sonship theology also explains why these groups rarely have schools devoted to training biblically qualified men and women but instead focus on students trained to operate in the miraculous. Franklin Hall expected believers to manifest as sons of God by operating in the power of the Spirit and performing miracles. Maxwell Whyte explains this progression of thought:

We are witnessing an outpouring of the Holy Spirit unparalleled in history. The church at large in the past has not been equipped with the power of God to do the work for which God created it. This power alone comes by the baptism in the Spirit which came on the day of Pentecost (Acts 2:4). It is for this reason that God is now pouring out His Spirit upon members of His church in both Protestant and Roman Catholic sections. [31]

A faulty Christology inspired this sonship movement to focus on the supernatural works of God more than the historic gospel message of repentance and sanctification. Holiness and spiritual maturity run a

---

[30] Hall, *Atomic Power With God.*

[31] H. A. Maxwell Whyte, "A Body Thou Prepared Me," *New Wine Magazine* 1, no. 3 (November 1969): 1, accessed December 11, 2017, https://csmpublishing .org/wp-content/NewWineArchives/Full_Issues/1969/NewWineMagazine_Issue _11-1969.pdf

dis-tant second to the importance of demonstrating power through mystic-miracles. As can be expected this teaching is seen throughout Bill Johnson's books and sermons. Just like Branham and Hall of the Latter Rain order, modern prophets and apostles of the NAR advocate for a spiritual super-race of Christians who hold dominion over the earth and usher in the kingdom of Christ.

Before I [Anthony] came to understand the theological issues at play, I witnessed an application of this "patristic" super-system while hosting a television show on TBN early in my ministry career. Before the show, Paul Crouch Sr., formidable founder of TBN, walked into the green room providing courteous greetings to all. But attached to his shoulder was a young man around twenty years old. And when I say "attached to his shoulder," I mean literally attached. The young man's job was to follow the "father" wherever he went, one hand always on Crouch's shoulder, ready to serve him like a butler during Southern slave trade or a courtesan of the Roman empire. In the vernacular, it was downright "creepy" so I quickly walked out and never looked back. I've since come to learn that this type of servitude by "young lads" is quite common for power-players in the prosperity movement.

After two world wars, the persistence of regional famine, terrorism, and ongoing threat of nuclear war, many realize the foolishness of promising an earthly kingdom now. Yet, aside from the obvious social absurdity of accepting this new theology, there are two fundamental biblical flaws in a Kingdom Now position: (1) the observed corruption of the world implies that somehow God has lost control; and (2) God needs man to help him regain what he has lost. The Bible teaches neither idea. The Bible does *not* teach that God lost control of His creation. The Bible does *not* teach man is the agent to salvage God's plan. The Bible does *not* teach earth will grow increasingly better. Quite the contrary, the Bible explicitly states that man failed his original purpose by falling into sin. Only when Jesus came as God made flesh, was *He* was able to perfectly obey the Father's original purpose; He is "crowned with glory," given "all authority in heaven and earth," and all " things [are] under His feet," allowing us to "one day reign with Him on His throne" (Heb 2:9; Eph 1:22; Rev 3:21).[32]

---

[32] This is of course customary of premillennial eschatology.

The Bible is clear that God is sovereign over the universe and holy over all things for all time (Psa 115:3; Isa 46:10). All things extend from His divine plan and not one atom moves without His sustaining will. The idea that God is simply waiting for faithful men or women to speak God's plan into existence is heretical. This power *belongs to God alone*. He is intolerant of attempts to usurp His authority: "I am God, and no other is God, even none like Me, declaring the end from the beginning" (Isa 46:8-11; 14:27).[33]

Doctrinal Error #4: The Dichotomy of Scripture & Spirit

Joel Beeke, in his article about Calvin's knowledge and piety, summarizes his view of Calvin's teaching about the work of the Holy Spirit and the written Word this way: "The work of the Spirit does not supplement or supersede the revelation of Scripture, but authenticates it."[34] The 1978 *Chicago Statement on Biblical Inerrancy*, Article XVII reads, "We affirm that the Holy Spirit bears witness to the Scriptures . . . We deny that this witness of the Holy Spirit operates in isolation from or against Scripture."[35] For nearly 100 years American evangelicals have affirmed the ancient teaching of the church that God's Word is the primary vehicle through which the Holy Spirit chooses to speak. This isn't what Bill Johnson teaches. A common tagline at Bethel Church is: "Don't keep God in a box" and for Bill Johnson this means God likes to talk outside of His written Word. The fourth error from Bill Johnson is diminishing of the power of God's Scripture in favor of a personal encounter—assumed to be with the Holy Spirit.

---

[33] What Johnson fails to recognize is that across the spectrum of evangelical Christianity, there are solid arguments for the literal return of Christ as the fundamental hope for all Christians. For further explanation the millennium see MacArthur and Mayhue, *Biblical Doctrine*, 171-173; and Grudem, *Systematic Theology*, 272, 539.

[34] Joel Beeke, "Calvin's Piety," *Mid-America Journal of Theology* 15 (2004): 40, accessed December 18, 2017, http://www.midamerica.edu/uploads/files/pdf/journal/15-beekepiety.pdf.

[35] International Council of Biblical Inerrancy, "The Chicago Statement on Biblical Inerrancy," Evangelical Theological Society, 1978, accessed December 18, 2017, http://www.etsjets.org/files/documents/Chicago_Statement.pdf.

As mentioned earlier, one hallmark of false teaching is twisting Scripture out of context to support a predetermined ideology or justify a personal experience. In scholarly circles this is often called "eisegesis"; when a reader or teacher imposes his or her ideas into a text instead of allowing the text to speak for itself. Throughout WHIE Johnson is guilty of such eisegesis. For example, in the first chapter Johnson contends that Romans 6:16 assumes Satan was empowered through some unknown agreement, that Luke 19:10 means Jesus' first advent recaptured man's dominion over physical earth, that Matthew 6:13 references victory over illness, that Revelation 3:7 stands for a "key" of David held by believers, that Matthew 25 is describing "miracle power" that was buried, and that Paul's words in Ephesians 3:20 ("all we ask or think") actually refers to signs and wonders. Johnson also gives no biblical support for a promise that the Heavenly Father ultimately wanted Satan defeated by mankind. None of the above statements were intended by the biblical writers nor supported by a wider reading of Scripture.

The most obvious and deceptive example of Johnsons' mishandling of Scripture is the false dichotomy he creates between the Bible and the Holy Spirit—as if the Holy Spirit would ever say something in contradiction to the Bible. Johnson repeatedly pits the Holy Spirit against the Bible by teaching that Scripture itself is insufficient to discern the voice of God. Johnson writes:

> Jesus did not say, "My sheep will know my book." It is His voice that we are to know. Why the distinction? Because anyone can know the Bible as a book—the devil himself knows and quotes the Scriptures. But only those whose lives are dependent on the person of the Holy Spirit will consistently recognize His voice. This is not to say that the Bible has little or no importance. Quite the opposite is true. The Bible is the Word of God, and scripture [sic] will always confirm His voice. That *voice gives impact* to what is in print. . . .[36]

It is important to see what Johnson says here: "The voice gives impact. . . ." Johnson has separated God's supposed voice from God's written Word, as if God will speak new information outside of what He has already promised (2 Tim 3:17). His assertion at the end that

---

[36] Johnson, *When Heaven Invades Earth*, 84.

"scripture [sic] will always confirm His voice" is misleading since we have already seen his willingness to manipulate the text to serve his own goals.

In subsequent pages, Johnson quips, "to follow Him we must be willing to follow off the map—to go beyond what we know."[37] He goes on to say, "signs have a purpose . . . they are not an end in themselves . . . they point to a greater reality . . . the sign is real . . . but it points to a reality greater than itself . . . We've gone as far as we can with our present understanding of Scripture. It's time to let signs have their place."[38] Time and again Johnson points to the authority of his so-called signs over and against the teaching of Scripture.

Johnson's emphasis on mystical-miracle signs that establish his authority above that of the Scripture is not far from a similar demonic plot which occurred 1,800 years ago by a heretical false prophet named Montanus.[39] Turner provides this salient summary, "Montanus, a zealous leader of the church, arose and called the church back to the primitive dynamism that characterized Pentecost. Thus arose the sect of Montanism in which the leader was sometimes viewed as the incarnation of the Holy Spirit."[40] While Johnson may not see himself as the incarnation of the Holy Spirit, he has followed in this tradition—and in the tradition of modern cult leaders like Joseph Smith who emphasized the burning bosom—which creates a signs-based experiential elitism that rises above Scripture.[41]

Is the Bible really nothing more than a road sign pointing us to the real voice of the Holy Spirit? Clearly, Jesus did not think so. When Jesus was on earth He taught His disciples through the Scriptures: "Then beginning with Moses and with all the prophets, He explained to them the things concerning Himself *in all the Scriptures*" (Luke 24:27, emphasis mine). Paul also taught this way: "So faith comes from hearing, and hearing *through the word* of Christ" (Rom 10:17; emphasis mine). In fact, orthodox Christianity has always taught that the Holy

---

[37] Ibid., 76.

[38] Ibid., 129.

[39] For study on the sect of Montanus, begin with Shelley, *Church History in Plain Language*, 64–66.

[40] George A. Turner, "Phrygia," in *Baker Encyclopedia of the Bible*, ed. Walter A. Elwell (Grand Rapids, MI: Baker Book House, 1988), 2:1693.

[41] Miller, *Promise of the Father*, 53.

Spirit chose to speak in the form of an objective and immutable canon; the Holy Spirit drives men by conscience and conviction back to those Scriptures for faith and practice.

So the question we must answer is this: Does the Holy Spirit speak to believers today? Yes. We think this is an important part of the Christian life. But we also recognize that His voice always leads us back to Scripture which is also his voice; a voice affirmed as our final authority and guide to faith by the Church for more than 2,000 years.

Like Jesus and like Paul, 2,000 years' worth of saints have embraced the Reformation concept of *sola Scriptura*. The Word of God written to us offers the power to change lives! One little verse, Romans 13:13, converted the immoral St. Augustine. The miserable monk Martin Luther was forever changed by Romans 1:17. For the American revivalist, Jonathan Edwards, it was 1 Timothy 1:17. Edwards said his first instance of inward delight was on reading, "Now unto the King eternal, immortal, invisible, the only wise God, be honor and glory forever and ever. Amen."

The Apostle Paul taught in 2 Timothy 3:16, "All scripture is inspired by God and profitable for teaching, for reproof, for correction, and for training in righteousness." The point is that Scripture *is* the means through which the Holy Spirit speaks; His word is not relative to any one person's experience nor is He a liar who would contradict the promises already spoken to us in Scripture. A regenerated life surrendered to the Holy Spirit will always point back to Scripture for faith, theology, and practice. Christianity has held this truth for 2,000 years, and no self-professed modern-day apostle or prophet should lead us away from this foundational truth.

Doctrinal Error #5: My Experience Proves My Truth

In a scenario similar to the adage, "which came first, the chicken and the egg?" we would be hard pressed to determine whether Johnson's version of the theology or his faith-healing methods came first. Either Johnson's faulty study paved the way for faulty practice or his desire to attract crowds gave rise to his faulty preaching. Either way, all of his errors culminate in one overarching theme that pervades all mystical-miracle heroes of the past and Bethel ministries and music today—*my experience defines my truth*. In essence, if "it" happened to me then, "it" must be from God.

As can be expected, the roots of "experience over truth" date back millennia. Historic Gnosticism was the belief that some people retain a secret, higher knowledge of spiritual matters and are, therefore, elite in their understanding and power. The church for centuries has rightly recognized this gnostic elitism as heretical; it's a divisive theology that destroys the bond of unity in Christ. Gnosticism contradicts and undermines the Gospel truth that every man and woman can have Christ to the fullest regardless of race, color, or creed.

> For all of you who were baptized into Christ have clothed yourselves with Christ. There is neither Jew nor Greek, there is neither slave nor free man, there is neither male nor female; for you are all one in Christ Jesus. And if you belong to Christ, then you are Abraham's descendants, heirs according to promise. (Gal 3:27-29)

In rebellion against this clear revelation from God, Johnson's Gnosticism roots itself in a personal revelation, linking his congregation to the heretical movements of the past and encouraging his followers to emulate them:

> Here's what I'm believing for—I know it's never happened, but I know that it must before the end. There must be, not just individuals—I'm thankful we have individuals that are rising up with such anointing, such strength, we have people scattered all over the planet right now that are just making a mess of things in all the right ways. We are so encouraged. But, what I'm believing for is a generation—a generation that'll rise up with a corporate faith, a corporate anointing to press into realms because it's my conviction that as much as God put on a William Branham, or a Kathryn Kuhlman, or a Wigglesworth, He'll put far greater anointing on a company of people than He ever would on an individual. To do that, there must be that corporate sense of, "we have to deal with the issue of obeying the rules of this kingdom to tap into the resources of this kingdom" . . . we cannot use the principles of this world and expect to tap into unlimited resource of the kingdom of God. . . .[42]

---

[42] Bill Johnson, "The Real Jesus - Part 4," posted September 2, 2010, accessed July 25, 2017, https://youtu.be/vHcRI60jOHI.

The sad outcome of this gnostic–experientialism is that Johnson's adherents have pursued his mission to its logical end. One frightening practice we see in Johnson's disciples is called "grave sucking";[43] going beyond Gnosticism to a form of necromancy. This is when people lie on the grave of a deceased individual (often one of the charismatic faith healers mentioned earlier in this book) in the hope of gaining "access to their Spirit power from the dead bones."[44] This is another formal heresy. As one can imagine, summoning dead spirits is something the Bible wholeheartedly condemns (Lev 19:26; 20:6; Deut 18:10; Gal 5:19–20; 1 John 4:1); God hates this practice endorsed by Johnson because it emphasizes the pursuit of power through dead human beings over and against the God who holds all power.

Conclusion

As stated in this chapter's introduction, there is no consistent or systematic biblical theology guiding Johnson's actions. Instead of the Scripture, he relies on human tradition alongside mystic-experience to advance his own brand of Kingdom Now dogma. At times convenient to his personal goals, he leans into pragmatism (if it works, it's true);[45] or accepts a more postmodern existentialism (if it's true for me, it's true).[46] This quasi-deconstructionism is summed up in the quest for

---

[43] It should be noted that while this abhorrent practice is connected to some of Bethel Church's members, Bill Johnson's direct involvement or condoning of it is not as direct. It appears that Johnson has never denied it taking place with people associated with Bethel, but he rejects the practice himself. According to Dr. Michael Brown, a noted Pentecostal leader and personal friend of Bill Johnson, Johnson denounced the practice of "grave sucking" on Brown's radio show, The Line of Fire (email correspondence with the editors, January 31, 2018). For Brown's entire interview of Johnson see, Michael Brown, host, "An Interview with Pastor Bill Johnson and Getting God's Mind in the Midst of Election Madness" (MP3 podcast), The Line of Fire with Dr. Michael Brown, posted October 12, 2016, accessed January 31, 2018, http://thelineoffire.org/2016/10/12/an-interview-with-pastor-bill-johnson-and-getting-gods-mind-in-the-midst-of-election-madness/.

[44] "Bethel Church Soaking Up the Anointing of the Dead, or Grave Sucking," posted December 8, 2011, accessed April 14, 2017, https://youtu.be/LrHPTs8cLls.

[45] John Herman Randall, Making of the Modern Mind: A Survey of the Intellectual Background of the Present Age (Boston, MA: Houghton Mifflin, 1940), 267.

power through personal experience. In the final analysis, Johnson lives out a self-justifying theology: everything extraordinary is from God, I experienced the extraordinary, therefore everyone who questions me is questioning God.

As Christians we must always sift our experiences through the refining truth of Scripture. Whenever we notice something supernatural or inexplicable, it demands a method for isolating, clarifying, and determining the true nature of that experience. If we fail to trust God's written Word to guide us and rely on ourselves as the final guide, we are in fact making ourselves into little gods.[47] Without the objective truth of God's written Word to guide each of us, we are set adrift and isolated from one another. If personal experience becomes our final guide to truth, no one is left who can discern what is a gift of God from what is a Trojan-horse attack from the devil, or from what is a lie from within our own heart.

Bill Johnson's sub-orthodox theology of Jesus, the Holy Spirit, the Bible, the Gospel, Christ's kingdom, and role of truth in a Christian's daily life is cloaked in powerful rhetoric and trite maxims but remains recognized heresy. Johnson continues to exhort this generation, "don't keep God in a box" of Scriptural truth. Bill Johnson, Bethel Church, the Third Wave, and the New Apostolic Reformation (NAR) define deception. They are the personification of the mystical-miracle movement. If we fail to speak out against this false doctrine, we will lose any sense of certainty in the God we worship and lose our true fellowship with one another.

---

[46] Jean-Paul Sartre, *Being and Nothingness: An Essay on Phenomenological Ontology* (New York, NY: Philosophical Library, 1956), 46.

[47] Millard Erickson, *Christian Theology*, 60.

7

True Healing

Introduction

J. I. Packer reminds us of this important truth, the Spirit's message is never "look at me" but always "look at Christ."[1] Proponents of the Third Wave/NAR make great noise about various influences of the Holy Spirit but in this chapter we will briefly examine the role of the Spirit and true healing as explained in Scripture.

When a doctor diagnoses a patient, the patient expects to be told the truth. A loving doctor will tirelessly search to identify the disease. When the disease is properly diagnosed, a prognosis is offered, and the doctor establishes a plan of treatment; then, and only then, can healing begin. J. R. Miller in his devotional book *More Than Cake*, offers this personal story on just how important suffering can be to the healing process. In a story titled, *When Love Conquers Compassion*, he writes:

> She walks her son down the long hospital hallway. People scurry about and take no notice of the suffering mother and child. Mattie holds firmly to his mom; in part to keep his balance, but mostly he wants to feel her warm hands in his own. "I'm tired mom. Please, I want to sit down;" but she does not let her son stop. He has to keep walking. He must exercise his limbs or his body will not heal. Only two days earlier Mattie was burned when a pot of boiling water was knocked from the stove; severely injuring his arm and leg. Pain now fills Mattie's three-year-old body, but his mother's love must force her son to walk. It takes every ounce of strength to resist the urge to pick up her son, to hold him, to comfort him, and to let him sit in his little red

---

[1] J. I. Packer, *Keep in Step with the Spirit: Finding Fullness in our Walk with God* (Grand Rapids, MI: Baker Books, 2005), 57.

wagon. If Mattie is to recover from his burns, love must conquer compassion. Holding back her tears, a mother's love must force her son to experience suffering. For Mattie, healing is on the other side of pain.

Where are you along life's path? Do you hurt? Does no one stop to notice your pain? In the darkest moments, you cry out to your god, "Where are you now! If you are real . . . if you are really loving . . . Where are you now when I need you the most!" Anger is a constant companion. Sorrow seems like the only escape from depression.

Only when your "god" becomes Father will you understand. Only when you experience a love that forces you to walk will you know rest. You must pass through the agony before the ultimate healing comes. Step after painful step; hold firm to the warm hand of the Father and know true love that conquers compassion.[2]

Just like Mattie's mom, if we hope to offer true healing, we must offer people the true medicine. Individuals addicted to the Third Wave/NAR experience are spiritually sick. Truth has become relative. Christ is portrayed as a means to a human-centered end and the Holy Spirit is a magic genie.[3] Obedience is regarded as legalism, biblical authority is deemed oppression, apostolic-doctrine is a four letter pejorative, and the absolute truth is a negotiable convenience depending on how it makes people feel. Healing those suffering under their oppressive doctrines won't come without some pain. God, the Great Physician, has a plan for healing already in place. Do we love God and love his children enough to implement our Father's best plan for healing?

As we've come to see through the preceding pages, these empty promises of a confused and short-lived healing simply leave the sick more diseased. The unnatural lust for signs and wonders can never quench our real thirst for the genuine work of the Holy Spirit. What we have seen over the years is that it only leaves people hopeless and smothered by deceit.

[2] J. R. Miller, *More Than Cake: 52 Meditations to Feed Your Teams* (San Diego, CA: Emerging Life Resources, 2011), 72-73.

[3] "Jenn on Holy Spirit," Bethel TV, posted March 1, 2009, accessed January 30, 2018, https://youtu.be/t5Ec_shJ-dk; start at 2:23.

For those in the asylum of Third Wave/NAR confusion there are steps that can be taken towards a path of true healing. First, learn to understand who the real Holy Spirit is from what the Scriptures teach about Him. Second, understand the focus and power promised by the Gospel of Jesus Christ. Finally, submit yourself fully to the sure revelation of God's written Word. In this final chapter, allow us to help guide those of you with an open mind, a willing heart, and a wounded spirit on this critical, and most likely difficult, journey to healing.

The Real Holy Spirit

The Holy Spirit is not an entertainer. He does not exist to put on a show. His aim is not to elevate men and women. He wants to point you to the person of Christ—not signs and wonders which pale in the light of His glory. He wants you to seek the Giver, not the gifts. Jesus' own words to the disciples in John 16 explain the Holy Spirit's divine job description.

The Spirit Convicts of Sin

The primary job of the Holy Spirit is to convict men and women of their sin. This means that whenever you see a church focused on repentance from sin and on submission to Christ you can be sure the Holy Spirit is at work. Conversely, if you find yourself in a setting where the Holy Spirit is on display, but the preachers and teachers are not urging people to mourn their sin and turn to Jesus in repentance, be cautious. Jesus Himself said, "And He, when He [the Holy Spirit] comes, will convict the world concerning sin" (John 16:8).

If a church or preacher ignores sin or tells people they are inherently good, the Holy Spirit is not involved. Love is why God sent His Son (John 3:16), but by His grace alone through faith we are saved and repentance is the evidence of genuine faith. If a Gospel message does not involve repentance, it's not the entire Gospel. The Holy Spirit regenerates a true believer and the evidence of regeneration is a sanctified life, fleeing from former sinful ways (1 Cor 6:11).

The Spirit Urges Righteousness

The Holy Spirit focuses on declaring Jesus as the righteous Son of God. Jesus explained, "and [the Holy Spirit] convicts concerning righteousness, because I go to the Father, and you no longer behold Me" (John 16:10).

Mankind needs salvation because sin separates him from God's holiness; it is an impassible gap that only the death and resurrection of Jesus Christ could restore. Jesus could not go to the Father unless He was sinless. Truly, Jesus was no mere man nor an anointed human. He was perfect; sinless through his virgin birth. And this Jesus without sin laid down His life, allowed men to condemn Him as a criminal and crucify Him in shame. But in the end, His perfect life and love were vindicated as the Father welcomed home His Son to sit at His right hand.

The Holy Spirit triumphantly declares Christ's righteousness, His deity, and that there is no condemnation for those who are given new life in Him (Rom 8:1). Jesus alone offered the cure that closes the impassable gap of sin between God and man and the Spirit applies that salve to our lives and testifies daily to our beautiful Savior.

The Spirit Exposes Satan

Jesus, full of the Holy Spirit, declares Satan a liar (John 8:44): a false ruler who wants us to reject the finished work of Christ and pursue the mystic-miracles of false apostles. At the heart of all who reject Christ rests the blinding and delusional power of darkness. Jesus affirmed, "and [the Holy Spirit] convicts concerning judgment, because the ruler of this world has been judged" (John 16:11).

The Holy Spirit is always involved in a Gospel message that confirms Satan as one who stands judged, pleading with sinful men declaring, "The accuser of the brethren is guilty!" (Rev 12:10). This good news is triumph for those who worship the risen Christ and tragedy for those who believe a different gospel or chase the fleeting prosperity of this world.

The Spirit Guides in Truth

The Holy Spirit guides every person into truth and never deception. People won't be led astray by the Holy Spirit nor spiritually abused by leaders who operate under His influence. Jesus told His disciples, "But when He, the Spirit of truth, comes, He will guide you into all the truth; for He will not speak on His own initiative, but whatever He hears, He will speak; and He will disclose to you what is to come" (John 16:13). These men, inspired by the Holy Spirit, would go on to write the New Testament so that every person could know the unchanging and unalterable truth that was once and for all delivered to the saints (Jude 3).

The Holy Spirit's revelation of God in the Scripture was, and is, sufficient. No further revelation is needed. The Holy Spirit is not involved in a gospel message that offers extra revelation to special individuals which, in its very existence, subverts the truth once and for all given to mankind. A gospel message that adds guarantees of mystical-miracles, faith-healing and financial prosperity to Scripture is a false gospel.

The Spirit Glorifies Christ

In many circles today, the Holy Spirit has become the centerpiece of sensationalistic church services and crusades. His so-called power is paraded around with blasphemous antics. Those responsible for putting false words into His mouth forget that He is the third member of the Godhead. Thereby, He will continue in His chosen and eternal role, elevating God the Father and God the Son. The Holy Spirit does not demand attention apart from people knowing His role and submitting to His work in their lives. His purpose on earth is to see Christ glorified above all else. Jesus declared, "He shall glorify Me; for He shall take of Mine, and shall disclose it to you" (John 16:14).

Divine revelation, breathed by the Spirit through the hands of faithful men, and recorded in the Bible was for the purpose of glorifying God and bringing the hope of salvation to all people. When the Bible is used to manipulate people, the name of Christ is tarnished. When the gifts of the Spirit are replaced by counterfeit displays of power, the name of Christ is tarnished. When the deity of Christ is twisted to fit a man-centered theology, His name is tarnished. The Holy Spirit is not involved in a gospel message that glorifies the gifts of men nor justifies the fallacies of their theology. He glorifies the Son for all that He is and ever will be (Heb 13:8).

The Real Gospel

The second step towards true healing is discerning what is real power unto soul transformation versus what is false power used for human gain.

People often wonder how a man or woman can be a false teacher if amazing signs accompany their ministry? Why would the devil be behind something that helps people feel better about themselves? Isn't the Gospel all about love, healing, restoration, and blessing? Sadly, many people will face the Lord Jesus one day and point to their resume of blessings, supposed signs, hit-or-miss prophecies, and big crowds as proof that they were preaching His name. He will not recognize them because they divorced themselves from His true Gospel in favor of their own version (Matt 7:21–23).

The Bible doesn't say anywhere that Gospel power is evidenced in monetary gain, a life without sickness, Twitter followers, or responses to an altar call. In fact, the Bible depicts the life of those faithful to the Gospel as likely to lead to poverty, abuse by authorities, and persecution. Jesus felt so strongly about this that He warned everyone they would need to love Him more than even their own mother and father (Matt 10:37). Paul proclaimed in Romans 1:16, "For I am not ashamed of the Gospel, for it is the power of God for salvation to everyone who believes." The point is that the power of God is the miracle of salvation; a dead sinner is regenerated!

God's power is ingrained in the Gospel message and cannot be presented as anything else. If the Gospel is presented as anything other than salvation from sin and the promise of eternal life, it is contaminated. The Gospel isn't married to temporal blessings, temporal healings, temporal relief from financial strain, or temporal possessions. Salvation is for the rich, the poor, the sick, the healthy, the marginalized, and the imprisoned. Even when saved, many will remain in humble circumstances. No amount of "naming or claiming by faith" can change that fact on this earth. Yet, Heaven will be full of eternal blessings for all who've come thirsty. That is the abundant life of eternal prosperity and ultimate healing we wait for (John 10:10).

The Real Scriptures

The final step of true healing is a commitment to the proper study, internalization, and obedience to all of Scripture. True faith in Christ is much more than mere knowledge of Christ, it means a fully dependent trust in Christ. This full dependence is a turning from sin and turning toward Christ. Such dependence will lead to a strengthened life through the Word of God: "So faith comes from hearing, and hearing by the word of Christ" (Rom 10:17).

In 2007, a high profile megachurch pastor had what he described as the "wake up call of his life" when he realized parts of his church were built on the power of strategy instead of the Scriptures. For 30 years his seeker-sensitive methods turned his church into a massive enterprise. Tens of thousands attended his uplifting sermons. People-centered programs kept everyone happily engaged in church life. As the numbers increased, it seemed that they were changing the world. However, when the church conducted a research survey to test the spiritual growth and member satisfaction rates, they found large portions of their congregation were biblically illiterate. The pastor and his leaders quickly realized that they had spent 30 years of their lives and millions of dollars going in the wrong direction. After publicly repenting, they expressed their need to establish the next 30 years of ministry on the foundation of Scripture.[4]

This experience is common in modern Christianity where people are made the center of the Gospel rather than Christ. In this messed-up system, the Bible serves as a nice side dish while the trendy music provides the main course. When we operate with man-centered passions it further proves that our view of God and view of ourselves is flawed. This way of thinking leads to long-term spiritual bondage—not true healing and freedom in Christ. The person living a gospel centered on himself or herself is living according to their own way. He has no hope of escaping his own depravity because he is living apart from the true power of God. The only solution to the problems we've laid out in this book is for each of us to read and understand what the Scriptures teach. The Bible teaches a lasting hope and healing because it offers enduring protection from those who seek to deceive. Physical healing cannot compare to the health of your soul. Look to God's Word for lasting relief.

Conclusion

If you've made it thus far, then we presume you are intrigued, if not wholly swayed about learning to trust in the primacy of Scripture

---

[4] Greg L Hawkins, and Cally Parkinson, *Move: What 1,000 Churches Reveal About Spiritual Growth* (Grand Rapids, MI: Zondervan, 2011), accessed December 19, 2017, https://www.willowcreek.com/move/Move_Forward_Ch1.pdf.

over experience. We pray you are committed to combating the counterfeits mentioned above. But for those who remain on the fence, allow us to offer one final part of God's healing plan . . . Love.

Yes, there may still be one reader who is still wondering: "Is it loving to say these things about so many apparently good people?" If that is you, wrestling internally with balancing truth versus tolerance and what it all means, allow us to ask one final question . . . Do you remember when Peter denied Jesus? In John 21, Jesus walked down the beach with Peter and, as you may recall, he asked Peter . . . "Do you love Me?" Then, the Lord followed up his series of questions with a very simple instruction, which he repeated three times: "Tend My lambs." "Shepherd My Sheep." "Tend My Sheep." Check that out! The obedient action that Christ commanded as evidence of His love was for his disciples to nourish and protect of His sheep . . . the church!

Dear friend, if Jesus restored his failed friend by demanding He protect the sheep, should not we also join in that mission? What does Jesus think about those who lie to, abuse, or manipulate His sheep? Wasn't it our Lord who said, "If anyone loves Me, he will keep my word; and My Father will love him, and We will come to him, and make Our abode with Him" (John 14:23)? Wasn't it the apostle John (who watched the scene unfold on the beach that day) who wrote, "By this we know that we love the children of God, when we love God and observe His commandments (1 John 5:2)? Ultimate love is following after Christ and helping others do the same.

At the beginning of this book we shared the story of a young man in a V-neck and skinny jeans claiming to be our church's next apostle and singing the praises of Bethel Church. Based on the evidence, do you believe he was an apostle? Do we need more revelation than what's contained in Scripture? Moreover, are the supposed signs and wonders at Bethel Church evidence of God's power or a demonic ploy?

We pray this book has clearly defined the deception of the mystical-miracle movement by using Bill Johnson and Bethel Church as our illustration. Our goal is that all true Christians will unite in demanding their repentance and resolve to protect the pure bride of Christ. We hope those caught in this deception will now find freedom and healing in the real Gospel of Jesus Christ. This book was published just a few months after the celebration of the 500th anniversary of the Protestant Reformation. In light of those who stood for truth in subsequent generations, we close with the words of famed reformer Martin Luther:

> [The preacher] should open his mouth vigorously and confidently, to preach the truth that has been entrusted to him. He should not be silent or mumble but should testify without being frightened or bashful. He should speak out candidly without regarding or sparing anyone, let it strike whomever or whatever it will. It is a great hindrance to a preacher if he looks around and worries about what people like or do not like to hear, or what might make him unpopular or bring harm or danger upon him. As he stands high on a mountain in public place and looks around freely, so he should also speak freely and fear no one.[5]

---

[5] Martin Luther, *The Sermon on the Mount and the Magnificat*, Luther's Works, ed. Jaroslav Pelikan, Hilton C. Oswald, and Helmut T. Lehmann (Saint Louis, MO: Concordia Publishing House, 1999), 21:9.

Appendix 1

Rescued From Deception

When I [Costi] first became aware of the deception I was saved from, I was sitting in my office studying for a sermon on John 5:1–17. As I made textual observations and then turned to a commentary for further digging, the tears began to flow from my eyes and drip down onto the MacArthur commentary I was using. Everything became so obvious in that moment as I noticed things about Jesus that I had never thought before. I repented, turned to Christ, and thanked Him for opening my eyes to the truth. Like countless others, I wrote a "thank you" letter to Grace to You, and, surprisingly, I received a voicemail from John MacArthur. It was the worst "missed-call" I have ever experienced! Still, I'll never forget his words in it: "Costi, your story reminds me of what we read about in the book of Jude. You were snatched from the burning." His reference made me laugh out loud with joyful gratitude to the Lord for His power to save. Since then, I've had the privilege of receiving many emails, tweets, and phone calls from people as well. These people aren't thanking me for anything I've done (because in fact I've done nothing), but rather, they are telling me that Jesus of the Bible saved them too! It's like a family reunion of long lost foster kids who find each other as adults. It's an endless stream of believers from far and wide saying, "We're family! We're family!"

When we started working on this book it got me [Costi] thinking: *What if we had an appendix with some of those messages from people? It would be a small monument to God that showcases His mercy and grace to us kids.* After such an arduous journey through the mire of false teaching, it's likely that we all could use a "pick me up" so I'm glad we have this to offer you. May it encourage you and be a praiseworthy memorial to God. He has snatched us all from the burning.

The following testimonies were submitted by real people who have been saved by the grace of God. Each one serves as a reminder that God uses faithful ministries and ministers as His means of bringing about salvation for the lost (Rom 10:14–17). Every story is verified, names have not been changed, and locations show that God is rescuing His people all around the world. Deception is widespread, but the power of the true Gospel cannot be thwarted.

I'm an ORU grad, and former Methodist. My church started introducing the Brownsville revival footage right before I graduated high school to go to ORU. I was there when Richard Roberts was at the helm. My husband and I were very oppressed by Word of Faith teaching on tithing, seed faith, and speak things into existence. We were never content with our lot in life, and we were always sowing into ministries (700 Club, Perry Stone, Rod Parsely) on top of tithing. All the while we were going deeper into debt. We were set free after watching a "Wretched" video by Todd Friel on YouTube of a pastor calling out a self-appointed prophetess. That led us to a video of John MacArthur rebuking Joel Osteen. We were hooked. We watched sermon after sermon of John MacArthur, which prepped us just in time for his Strange Fire Conference. The Lord had graciously prepared our hearts to receive that message, and draw us both to deep repentance. We are so humbly grateful for the faithful ministry of John MacArthur, Phil Johnson, Justin Peters, Steve Lawson, James White, Chris Rosebrough, Todd Friel, Alistair Begg, RC Sproul, David Platt, Mike Abendroth, and so many more! Most of all, to Jesus for His mercy in saving us! Now, my husband is a fervent student of the Word of God, and is currently helping with biblical counseling in our Bible church here in Oklahoma. **Amy, 38, Tulsa, Oklahoma**

My academic background is philosophy and theology. How did I end up in a Word of Faith church? Sadly, I suffer from depression. I had been involved for years in Charismatic churches. During one dark period of my life my mood took a nosedive and I ended up in a very vulnerable place. My wife and I got an invitation to a Word of Faith church and in my fragile mental state I became convinced that they had the answer to my mental health problems. I could speak the Bible out into my life and command by mind to be well. The trouble is – the health & wealth theology doesn't deliver. It didn't work for me, and it didn't work for an elder in that church who ended up dying of cancer – a physical and spiritual wreck. After witnessing some ugly spiritual abuses and manipulation we left that church after two years. Gradually my mental health returned as I began to see the fullness of the true gospel again. God guided me to the work of men such as Justin Peters, and I have since felt a calling to challenge Word of Faith doctrine wherever it raises its ugly head. **Stephen, 39, Belfast, Ireland**

In 2014, I became a shut-in due to a medical condition. It was then that I came upon recordings of John MacArthur's "Strange Fire", Justin Peter's "Clouds Without Water" series, and Ray Comfort's "Hell's Best Kept Secret." God not only delivered me out of fourteen years of false conversion, He systematically delivered me from every false teaching that I had been deceived by such as: Word of Faith, Health & Wealth/Prosperity Gospel, mysticism, and a few others. In a providential way, God used my affliction to keep me shut in and away from my doctrinally corrupt church. Two years later, a quick and unexpected move to a different city placed me close to a wonderfully biblical church. As I write this testimony, my Geneva Bible rests beside me. If it were not for God's mercy, I would be still deceived and most likely reading the Joyce Meyer Bible. Praise the Lord! **Pamela, 43, Ontario, Canada**

My husband and I did not grow up in Christian households and had few Christian friends. When God opened our eyes and saved us, we both had come to faith in Jesus by reading the scriptures alone at home. We certainly didn't have a mature understanding of the Bible but believed in Jesus and were compelled to be baptized. We began attending a charismatic church, and kept reading our Bibles diligently. Soon, as we witnessed excessive scripture-twisting tactics, we knew it was time to leave. At first, it shipwrecked our young faith because we couldn't understand why the teaching and practice didn't match the scriptures. For sometime, we couldn't step foot into another church again. Eventually my husband introduced me to R.C Sproul and Ligonier Ministries. From there, our lives were changed forever. We found a biblically faithful church soon after and have never looked back! **Sylvia, 27, Melbourne, Australia**

I was "saved" at 16 years of age and baptized by a Pentecostal preacher, a woman, in her bathtub. She was the mother of my step-mother. This family had get-togethers where they prophesied to each other and I was always pressured to seek the "baptism of the Holy Spirit." I prayed, begged, pleaded and pretty much everything but stand on my head. I spent years in condemnation and questioning my faith. I finally just gave up. I am so thankful that God did not allow me or my husband to stay in our ignorance. My journey out of the WOF/NAR /Prosperity movement started with a Jay Adams book, which led to Voddie Baucham sermons online, which led to John MacArthur online, including "Strange Fire", and many other Biblical teachers. After a long search, we are now members of a Reformed Baptist church. After so many years of being told to get my mind out of the way and listening to what I call "cotton candy" messages; all sugar, no sustenance, it is refreshing to hear the "meat" of the Word week in and week out. *Tami, 51, Willis, Texas*

I was raised in a non-denominational church that thrived on health and wealth theology. Speaking things into existence was what it was all about! Our pastor got a new Porsche every spring and had deacons appointed to keep church members from talking to him after the services. My father was one of his deacons for a while but we left the church after a while. I discovered John MacArthur and Justin Peters through my new pastor in our Baptist church. Unfortunately, my father is still following teachers like Creflo Dollar, Jesse Duplantis, and many others. Some of my best friends are really big followers of Benny Hinn and Kenneth Copeland and one has sadly become an "Apostle." My wife and I wasted a lot of time and money on deceptive theology but we are thankful to be walking in truth now. *Clint, 27, Texarkana, Texas*

I wasn't connected to a traditional church. I was a part of a house church movement. The teachings were closely related to that of the New Apostolic Reformation. The idea was that we could experience miracles like instantaneous healing or even raise the dead if we "prayed in the Spirit" long enough. Everyone was supposed to prophecy and receive extra biblical revelation. I was made to feel as though I was not growing in the Lord if I didn't have a revelatory dream or prophetic word. It caused me to manufacture prophetic words that I thought were from the Lord. It wasn't until I didn't get the healing I desired that I began to question why we didn't look like the church as it was described in scripture. Soon I realized that my beliefs, and our supposed church was a mockery. After that I became alone and lonely. I cried out to God for truth – I begged Him. Providentially I came across a Paul Washer sermon and my life changed completely. Shortly after that eye-opening moment, God provided a doctrinally sound church that has been a great blessing to me. *Yolanda, 32, Raeford, North Carolina*

In 2003, I was a teen who began getting involved in a Word of Faith church. We practiced things such as tongues, healing, prosperity, and stayed in it until 2010. Many confusing things occurred that were awkward during my time there. After the pastor passed away, the church went downhill from there with his wife leading the church. Many services were full of things are found nowhere in the Bible like holy laughter for the entirety of a service instead of preaching, to tongues that were just people repeating the phrase, "Hot dog, hot dog." I ended up leaving there to go in the Army and over the course of five years, I abandoned those practices. After leaving the Army in 2015, I began studying God's word and He opened my eyes to truth. I have many family members still caught up in the Word of Faith movement. **Mark, 25, Gardner, Massachusetts**

I got saved at a hip charismatic church. Besides forgiveness of sins, we were taught that Jesus died for our health and abundant life; that we needed to tithe, give, serve and speak only positive words in order to be blessed. One failed marriage later, I began to wonder why my life wasn't bearing much good fruit. The pastoral couple had a TV show, preached sermons on relationships and sex, but were hardly available to counsel. Blaming myself, I resolved to follow Jesus even more fervently, which lead me straight into a heavily NAR-influenced congregation. They taught that we would be outside of God's will if we failed to follow directions revealed only to our "prophetic" elders. Something didn't feel quite right. It was time to change strategies. So, I actually open the Bible and seek out the truth concerning biblical teachers. Pirate Christian Radio was a huge blessing to my growth. After a brief disillusionment, I abandoned the "different gospel" (Gal.1-6) I had followed. **Daniela, 43, Gig Harbor, Washington**

My husband and I were saved out of the charismatic and Word of Faith movement 7 years ago. The Lord used Ray Comfort's "good person cartoon" to present the gospel to me and I repented and believed. Then my husband and I started listening to Todd Friel, who then led us to John MacArthur and RC Sproul. From there, we began to understand theological truths more than ever before. In the years that have followed, God has continued to grow us in His truth and we have been trying to reach those and still in the Word of Faith movement. **Callie, 33, Bonham, Texas**

Oddly enough I was raised in a Mennonite church that leaned towards various charismatic practices. I accepted Jesus into my heart when I was 6 and lived as a false convert until early adulthood. (I am now 33) We had services with people speaking in tongues and even getting slain in the spirit. It was a *confusing time for me but I went along with it because I thought it was "normal". The times I remember most are the youth retreats where if you did not get "filled" with the spirit or speak in tongues you were looked at as abnormal. So sadly on those trips I faked it. It was easy enough because I could watch their behavior and imitate it. I left that church at 16 and was eventually saved at 19. About 6 years ago I learned the reformed faith and have been growing ever since.* **Marcus, 33, Easton, Pennsylvania**

[But you, beloved,] . . . have mercy on some, who are doubting; save others, snatching them out of the fire; and on some have mercy with fear, hating even the garment polluted by the flesh. Now to Him who is able to keep you from stumbling, and to make you stand in the presence of His glory blameless with great joy to the only God our Savior, through Jesus Christ our Lord, be glory, majesty, dominion and authority, before all time and now and forever. Amen. (Jude 22-25)

Appendix 2

Frequently Asked Questions

Q: Does God "speak" to people apart from the Bible?

A: Some evangelicals assert that God "speaks" to His people today apart from the Bible. Most do not make the bold assertion that God speaks "authoritatively" as He did in biblical times but instead explain a new version of "fallible prophecy" that includes visions, dreams, voices, and words of knowledge.[1]

When asked about this issue, we must first determine what each person intends when they say, "God speaks to me." Some well-intended Christians have used this term to simply describe their intuitive guiding, prompting, or impression from the Holy Spirit toward an act of righteousness or wisdom. This position would be considered the "mind of Christ" (1 Cor 2:16) and be completely normative for Christians who are filled with the Spirit and being led by the Spirit (Eph 5:18; Rom 8:14). This is well within the boundaries of historic Christian orthopraxy.

However, there are others, as mentioned above, who use the term "God speaks to me" in reference to new forms of prophecy, visions and dreams, also called, "Words from the Lord." Proponents of this view, who find their chief support in 1 Corinthians 14:29 and 1 Thessalonians 5:20-22, must reassess their position. A simple reading of these passages *might* suggest Paul is requesting the church "pass judgment" (*diakrino*) on prophecies, telling congregants to discern which are truthful and which erroneous; however, if the unidentified object in each text is not the "prophecy" but the "prophet" himself then each verse aligns with the larger portion of Scripture and simply teaches that each congregation was to assess whether a person giving a message was true or false (i.e. Deut 13:1-5; Matt 7:15-20; 1 John 4:1-

---

[1] See Wayne Grudem, *The Gift of Prophecy in the New Testament and Today* (Westchester, IL: Crossway, 1988), 74-79; cf. 104-5.

6; Rom 16:17–19). This is a much simpler and more consistent interpretation and fits within the larger teaching of Scripture that God's written Word is authoritative. We must contend that anytime "God speaks" it is always 100% accurate and not up for debate.[2]

The Word of God was declared by Christ Himself and propagated by special apostles designated to write it (Heb 1:1–2; 2:3–4; Matt 16:15–19; John 14:26; Eph 2:19–20). So, the church now lives by *sola Scriptura* and to tamper with this central truth invites a host of theological and practical problems. Anything that diverts a Christian's attention, joy, memorization, meditation, and reliance away from Scripture must be rejected.

Q: Should a true Bible teacher share a stage with a false teacher?

A: No biblically qualified teacher should ever share a stage to support a false teacher or do a conference with a false teacher. The only exceptions for sharing the stage would be that a partnership has been forged to allow the false teacher to announce their public repentance (the ultimate goal), or the biblical teacher plans to publicly rebuke the false teacher and his audience. If a Bible teacher does this, he will likely not be invited back. Therefore, if a man or woman continues to be invited into fellowship with false teachers, it is most likely because he or she is theologically confused about the truth. In essence, they have neglected one of the primary duties of a disciple—to glorify God.

Q: Should I seek Baptism of the Holy Spirit?

A: No, Acts 1:5 references the Baptism *in* the Holy Spirit. The Greek usage of the punctiliar passive future means one particular time. In essence Jesus said, "Very soon [ten days from now] this special one-time-only-event will occur." Subsequently, the Jews were baptized by the Holy Spirit in Acts 2, the Samaritans in Acts 8, the Greeks in Acts 11, and the followers of John the Baptist in Acts 19. First, we must know that Jesus was the agent of the baptism and the Spirit was the element. The passive voice used in the Greek phrase means this isn't something

---

[2] For further analysis, see John H. Armstrong, *The Coming Evangelical Crisis: Current Challenges to the Authority of Scripture and the Gospel* (Chicago, IL: Moody Press, 1996), 77–89.

anyone was told to look for, ask for, beg for, mumble for, heal for, sing emotional music for, or climb Mount Everest for, it was 100% a divine and sovereign gift. Next, we must note it was a completed baptism. 1 Corinthians 12:13 says, "By one Spirit we were all baptized into one body, Jews or Greeks, slaves or free, and we were all made to drink of one Spirit." The passive aorist means *past* fact in the life of every believer. ALL who have been saved by Christ Jesus have been baptized. The Spirit's baptism is not some post-conversion experience to be craved, but an historical fact in the life of every disciple to be praised. Finally, this means that all believers today, and in every age, are immediately baptized in the Spirit upon conversion. 1 Corinthians 6:17 says, "the one who joins himself to the Lord is one spirit with Him." The moment that a person comes to saving faith in Christ, they are recipients of the Holy Spirit. As Miller writes:

> The Promise [of Spirit Baptism] is clear, the hope is real, now let us embrace our Father's covenant-love and live boldly in the power of his Holy Spirit granted to every believer of every age. Let us not fear being left out of God's sovereign work of grace. Let us cease to divide the church with false tradition, and let us unite as the People of His sure Promise of power. [3]

So, if we are all baptized in the Spirit and have the full promise of God, why do certain people seem to have more of the Holy Spirit? While there is one baptism, there are many fillings of the Holy Spirit. His filling depends upon a daily obedience to God's Word and surrender to God's way (Acts 5:32).

Q: Should any true Christian share or support Bethel Music?

A: No. Regardless of how good the music sounds it's a poisonous mixture of truth and error that is used to validate Bill Johnson's false teaching and his church. Benny Hinn's music isn't played on main-stream radio, so why is Bethel's? They are both false teachers of Jesus Christ. Some may argue that it sounds good and makes people feel good. So does junk food until it clogs your arteries.

---

[3] J. R. Miller, *Have You Not Yet Received the Spirit?*, 44.

Q: When is it okay for a true Christian to intermingle with those who are involved in this type of false movement?

A: As explained earlier, false teachers should be avoided completely. As for followers, each person must use discernment to decide at what level a healthy relationship can be maintained without bringing reproach on the name of Christ. Varying views on baby baptism or church music styles are not as important as allowing false teachings about Christ to fill our minds and churches. Every Christian should strategically use Jude's counsel in verses 22-23.

Q: What does "Touch Not My Anointed" in Psalms 105:15 mean?

A: This is an oft-used phrase in charismatic circles to scare Christians from pointing out errors of theology or lifestyle. But, like every other Bible verse, it is a twisted use of the text. In the era of Israelite monarchy, no one was allowed to kill or commit a violent physical act against anointed kings or prophets. David made this prohibition famous when he wouldn't kill Saul. He quoted God saying, "Do not touch my anointed ones, and do My prophets no harm" (Psa 105:15). In 1 Samuel 24:10-11 when David had the chance to kill Saul (and some would say rightfully so), he cries out to Saul, "Behold, this day your eyes have seen that the LORD had given you today into my hand in the cave, and some said to kill you, but my eye had pity on you; and I said, 'I will not stretch out my hand against my lord, for he is the LORD's anointed." This command and the many other similar passages surrounding the situation with David and Saul had to do with David (or his men) not killing Saul—the Lord's anointed king. Modern day prosperity preachers and fake healers can attempt to turn this into a timeless principle or make it about not challenging their teaching, however, their efforts cannot stand up to what Scripture actually teaches. It makes no sense and has no power when they use it against anyone speaking the truth about their errors.

Furthermore, no one should fear dishonest prophets or those claiming to be prophets. If some prosperity prophet ignores context and spouts Old Testament commands to control people in the church age, they'd better be prepared to face God's standard for a prophet as described in Deuteronomy 18:18-23:

"I [God] will raise up a prophet from among their countrymen like you, and I will put My words in his mouth, and he shall speak to them all that I command him. It shall come about that whoever will not listen to My words which he shall speak in My name, I Myself will require it of him. But the prophet who speaks a word presumptuously in My name which I have not commanded him to speak, or which he speaks in the name of other gods, that prophet shall die.' You may say in your heart, 'How will we know the word which the Lord has not spoken?' When a prophet speaks in the name of the Lord, if the thing does not come about or come true, that is the thing which the Lord has not spoken. The prophet has spoken it presumptuously; you shall not be afraid of him."

Q. What does "By His stripes we are healed" in Isaiah 53:5 mean?

A. This is perhaps the most famous verse for Word of Faith preachers to claim as an all-encompassing promise to the sick. They use it in the sense that people should be physically healed right now on earth. An improper interpretation and understanding of this passage is devastating to millions of people who think something is wrong with their faith because they aren't healed as promised. Several truths emerge when we rightly divide the Word of Truth. Firstly, the entire chapter of Isaiah 53 is primarily salvific—meaning it is focused on the atonement of Christ having saved sinners from the wrath of God. Isaiah writes that Christ was, "pierced through for our transgressions, He was crushed for our iniquities; the chastening for our well-being fell upon Him, and by His scourging we are healed" (Isa 53:5). This healing is not from physical sickness: it's clearly from sin. This verse does not teach that Christians have an earthly right to be physically healed as many wrongly teach, but that Christians have an earthly right to be justified by faith and look forward to life after death in Heaven. In fact, if this was a blanket promise that all sickness would be healed on earth, then no Christian would ever be sick today, hospitals would be empty of believers, and the Apostle Paul himself would not have "left Trophimus sick at Miletus" (2 Tim 4:20) or had a bodily illness of his own (Gal 4:13–14). It is a cruel lie when false teachers (or well-meaning but erroneously taught Christians) quote Isaiah 53:5 to explain that physical healing is guaranteed here on earth. While God does in fact still heal people today, He does so according to His sovereign will—for His purposes and glory. So the question begs to be asked, was physical healing provided for in the atonement? The answer is a resounding yes! So much so that even Peter quotes Isaiah 53:4 when Jesus healed his mother-in-law and "all who were ill" in Matthew 8:16-17. A moment like that fulfilled such a prophecy and proved that Jesus was in fact the Christ who had the power to heal all. The complete realization of Isaiah 53:5 rests on the fact that it is an eternal promise much like the promise of eternal life, the glorified body we receive as described in 1 Corinthians 15:40-51, and great heavenly rewards for our service to Christ on earth as explained in 1 Corinthians 3:11-14. Because of Christ's resurrection, there are numerous blessings we will enjoy in Heaven as *guaranteed*, but we are to trust His sovereignty through the trials we experience on this earth; looking forward to the hope and healing of Heaven. The atonement means that when we are in Heaven we will not be sick, we will not decay, and we will not experience pain—all will be perfect as promised. That is God's will.

Q: Isn't Jesus "the same yesterday, today, and forever" according to Heb-rews 13:8?

A: The entire chapter of Hebrews 13 isn't difficult to understand contextually. While verses 18-25 are filled with personal instructions for prayer, obedience, and an update on Timothy, we will look specifically at verses 1-17. Overall, verses 1-17 are an exhortation to perform Christian duties such as brotherly love (13:1), being kind to strangers (13:2), remembering those in prison (13:3), being faithful in marriage (13:4), and being free from the love of money (13:5). It is verse 7 that provides us the reason for the famous declaration of verse 8. Hebrews 13:7 reads, "Remember those who led you, who spoke the word of God to you; and considering the result of their conduct, imitate their faith." The exhortation here is that when living the Christian life, they ought to draw encouragement from their former leaders. It was these leaders who first and foremost led by example, and above all their example was founded on speaking the Word of God. The writer then tells them to consider the result of their conduct. In a nutshell, he tells them to look at the fruit of their leaders lives and emulate them. Homer Kent, former professor at Grace Theological Seminary writes,

> Eventually these leaders had passed from the scene. It need not be
> inferred that they all died a martyr's death, although they may

have. The real importance was that all had been faithful to the end. None had wavered and given up faith in Christ. Let these readers continue imitating that steadfast example.[4]

With a clear understanding of the author's intentions and the surrounding context, we come to the famous verse 8: "Jesus Christ *is* the same yesterday and today and forever." Why would the writer have felt the need to remind the readers that Jesus is the same yesterday, today, and forever? To promise miracles? Verse 9 reveals the purpose, "Do not be carried away by varied and strange teachings; for it is good for the heart to be strengthened by grace, not by foods, through which those who were thus occupied were not benefitted." There it is—Christ is explained as unchanging because live-saving truth was forever established in Him. False teachers had begun to infiltrate the church and introduce false doctrines about Christ, and many Judaizers linked the works of the law to salvation. In order that his audience might find security in the unchanging work of Christ on the cross, the author of Hebrews exhorts them with the unchanging nature of Jesus in verses 8 and 9. John MacArthur comments, "The Jews were used to having religious regulations for every-thing, and it was hard for them to adjust to freedom in Christ."[5] The Letter to the Hebrews, and contextually speaking, chapter 13, has no-thing to do with miracles, signs and wonders, or the works of men. It has everything to do with who Jesus was, is, and forever will be.

Q: Isn't it always God's will to heal if we have enough faith?

A: No greater burden is placed on people than what we've already covered in previous chapters—that if you just have enough faith you can get your healing. On his website Johnson writes:

> How can God choose not to heal someone when He already purchased their healing? Was His blood enough for all sin, or just certain sins? Were the stripes He bore only for certain illnesses, or certain seasons of time? When He bore stripes in His body He made

---

[4] Homer Kent, *The Epistle to the Hebrews* (Grand Rapids, MI: Baker Book House, 1972), 281.

[5] John MacArthur, *Hebrews*, MacArthur New Testament Commentary (Chicago, IL: Moody Publishers, 1983), 437.

a payment for our miracle. He already decided to heal. You can't decide not to buy something after you've already bought it.[6]

Though no specific passage of Scripture is used to back up Johnson's definite claim, a misuse of Isaiah 53:5 tends to be the main proof text for this type of statement. Asking such questions as he has would be akin to asking, "Was his death on the cross not enough to give eternal life? Why are we still living on earth then?" The logic is untenable and his appeal to power is powerless. The Bible teaches the exact opposite of Johnson's twisted theology. John 5:1–17 describes a man at the pool of Bethesda who had no faith, did not even know who Jesus was, and yet he was healed. There were countless other sick people surrounding the pool, but Jesus chose to heal just one. Was He unloving then to the rest? Was He not the Son of God since He did not heal every person? God is sovereign in healing, and He does not heal all, all the time. When He does heal, it is not because one person has great faith and another has little faith, but always by His power and for His glory. The answer we provide here is a threat to the mystical-miracle workers, because it weakens the power from their pulpits, it removes money from their pockets, and it demolishes the foundations of their theology. Sadly, this may be too much for most to sacrifice for the real Jesus Christ.

Q: What does Matthew 7:1 mean, "Judge not lest you be judged?"

A: Matthew 7:1 has nothing to do with prohibiting Christians from discerning good theology from bad or from holding to account a false teacher. This passage is concerned with those who would judge others in hypocrisy like Pharisees. The Pharisees believed they were better than others simply by their self-determined standards—not biblical ones. In today's terms, this would be like a prosperity preacher having a judgmental attitude towards a word of faith preacher—utter hypocrisy! When Jesus says, "For in the way you judge, you will be judged; and by your standard of measure, it will be measured to you" (Matt 7:2), He is saying that God will judge us with the same type of judgment that we ourselves use to judge others. When Bible believing Christians weigh

---

[6] "Is It Always God's Will to Heal Someone?" Bill Johnson Ministries, Q&A, accessed January 8, 2018, http://bjm.org/qa/is-it-always-gods-will-to-heal-someone/.

the false teachings of a ministry or minister, they are not violating Matthew 7, rather, they are judging by the standard with which every teacher should be judged (James 3:1). When faithful preachers call out false teachers based on the standard of God's Word, they are rightly judging. In no way is Matthew 7:1-2 a prohibition against calling out false teaching. We are to expose deeds of darkness (Eph 5:11) and mark those who cause divisions through their false teaching (Rom 16:17-18).

Q: What is the prayer of healing mentioned in James 5?

A: Many of our English translations mention the healing of sickness in James 5. The word "sickness" is the Greek *astheneo* which in 13 of the 17 times it occurs in the epistles refers to spiritual affliction. The context of James clearly speaks of troubled believers wandering from the faith; so it seems most likely that James is referring to the restoration (Greek, *sozo*, meaning salvific rescue) of the soul and not a physical malady. Further evidence of this conclusion is found in the context of James 5 which includes the reference to "sins" (v. 15), "straying into apostasy" (v. 19), and "saving his soul from death" (v. 19). However, even if this passage is talking about prayer for physical healing, it gives clear guidelines that this prayer is not a sign-miracle from an apostles, but an act of the church's elders coming together to pray healing on a hurting person. In either case, this passage describes a community gathered out of compassion, not an audience gathered seeking a sign.

Appendix 3

Understanding Biblical Tongues

It is important to point out how rarely the Bible discusses any gift of signs, wonders, or tongues. While modern proponents of the sign-gifts preach signs, wonders, and tongues as evidence of genuine salvation and/or a special anointing, there is simply no biblical evidence to sup-port those claims. Even more surprising to some readers may be the relatively few mentions of spiritual gifts of any type. So before we can understand biblical tongues, it is helpful to understand the broader category of spiritual gifts.

Spiritual gifts are nowhere mentioned in the four Gospels. This is because spiritual gifts were not given to anyone until the church age began at Pentecost. Even then, the book of Acts does not offer any list of spiritual gifts. Acts describes some miraculous events, but without much explanation. It's only in four of the epistles where we are given any kind of list of what these gifts might be: Romans 12; 1 Corinthians 12–14; Ephesians 4, and 1 Peter 4; and the gifts described in these epistles aren't defined in terms of how they work. We see that these gifts are clearly given at conversion by the sovereign work of the Holy Spirit who baptizes every believer into Christ. Everyone who has the gift of the Holy Spirit is given some manifestation of His presence (or gifting) and it doesn't require pleading, emotion, or any form of ecstatic behavior.[1]

There is a common teaching within the Pentecostal/Charismatic tradition that every believer should seek certain gifts above others. Most notably, the theology that every believer should seek the gift of tongues as the highest expression of their spiritual vitality. This view is

---

[1] J. R. Miller, "One Gift; Many Giftings: The Supremacy of the Holy Spirit Over Every Spirit-Gifting" (paper presented at the Symposium on The Holy Spirit, Southern California Seminary, El Cajon, CA, July 27, 2015), 2–3, accessed January 9, 2018, http://www .morethancake.org /archives/9237.

largely based on a flawed reading of 1 Corinthians 12:31, "But earnestly desire the greater gifts. . . ." However, this verse specifies that the "greater gifts" are not tongues speaking, but the gifts of apostleship, prophecy, and teaching. Look back to verse 28 for this context, "God has appointed in the church, first apostles, second prophets, third teachers, then miracles, then gifts of healings. . . ." The words first, second, and third refer to priority of these gifts for advancing the mission of the church. Therefore, if Paul were telling believers to seek after a gift, it would be for the ones that enable missionary work or for the teaching of sound doctrine. However, the Greek word often translated desire isn't referencing an active seeking (as if someone can earn that gift with enough prayer). Instead, it is a word for jealousy, placed in a clause insinuating passion and zeal. In his seminal work *Miraculous Gifts*, Thomas Edgar writes,

> *Zeloo* is sometimes translated as covet or desire but a thorough study of *zeloo* indicates that it means to be zealous (KJV, ASV, NIV). Zeal for some, often implies desire. However, this meaning is derived from the context rather than the word itself. The entire section of 1 Corinthians (chapters 12–14) stresses the priority of the edifying gifts—apostle, prophet, and teacher—over the more spectacular gifts of tongues, which was apparently receiving undue emphasis at Corinth.[2]

In context, 1 Corinthians 12:31 urges the entire church (plural form) to be actively zealous for the missionary and teaching ministry. Paul is simply telling the Corinthians to be enthusiastic and passionate about the greater gifts, because those gifts edify the entire church above any one individual. These gifts, more than any other, help increase the bond of unity. This passage is not instructing believers to be unhappy with the gift already given to them by the Holy Spirit, but encouraging each person to accept the gift he's been given by God, while promoting the gifts of those who work to build the church. In other words, Paul is telling the Corinthians to stop all seeking after the same gift of tongues (which is being abused), and as a church body to desire that the other

---

[2] Thomas R. Edgar, *Miraculous Gifts: Are They For Today?* (Neptune, NJ: Loizeaux Brothers, 1983), 26. This appendix is largely a condensed view of Edgar's seminal work, *Miraculous Gifts*. For extensive study on classical cessationism we urge readers obtain a copy.

gifts be lifted up in order to restore the unity of the Spirit (which was lost by their lust for tongues). This then gives us a clear context for investigating the purpose of other miracles and sign-gifts (including tongues).

Biblical Miracles

Miracles in the Gospels

The only text in the Gospels which deals with an ongoing exercise of gifts after Pentecost is Mark 16:15-20,

> And He said to them," Go into all the world and preach the Gospel to all creation. He who has believed and has been baptized shall be saved; but he who has disbelieved shall be condemned. These signs will accompany those who have believed: in My name they will cast out demons, they will speak with new tongues; they will pick up serpents, and if they drink any deadly *poison*, it will not hurt them; they will lay hands on the sick, and they will recover.

In these verses, Mark clearly connects the miraculous signs with preaching the Gospel—demon casting, tongues, holding snakes, and drinking poison are all signs (*semeion*) performed in order to confirm Jesus and His words. Jesus said these signs would follow those who "believed." However, grammatically the antecedent "shall accompany" could either refer to those who had believed up until the time Jesus spoke it or to those who would believe in the future. Since both meanings are grammatically correct, the status of this promise must be derived from the context. The fact that Jesus made this statement to the apostles and referred to those "who had believed" (past aorist), implies the words were only for the early group of believers who had followed Him up until that point.

What cements this interpretation as correct is a simple analysis of the entire promise itself. Note, if the signs of tongues and healing are still present today, then so are the signs of snake handling and poison drinking. In essence, if this text applied to believers for all time, then no believer would ever die from drinking poison or a snake bite. The fact that this is an unconditional promise, not dependent on faith or crowds or trances (and without failure), proves it is a divine promise for a specific time. Furthermore, the Gospels continually develop the theme that Jesus healed when and how he chose, not based on the faith of people and often despite the faith of people (Matt 8:5-13; Mark 1:23-26; 9:17-29; Luke 17:11-19, John 5:1-16).

Clearly the Gospels describe a unique period of time as God on earth displayed His divinity, anointed select men to launch the church, and established Holy Scripture. When Jesus chose to heal He never failed, and He did not require the power of their "faith" to do so. His work was unique and should never be considered the normative experience or the expectation of church age believers.

Miracles in the Book of Acts

The book of Acts provides powerful descriptions of signs and wonders accomplished by the apostles to uniquely empower and set apart the early church. There are many miracles to note (Acts 2:1-14, 22; 3:3-16; 4:29-30; 5:1-10; 6:8; 8:6-13; 9:1-18, 32-42; 13:11-12; 14:3, 8-10; 19:11-12; 20:9-12, 17-38).

A cursory reading of the book will show that the events of Acts are far different from the supposed miracles within Third Wave/NAR circles today. Note these clear differences:

1. The miracles were performed mostly by apostles.
2. The miracles were performed upon unbelievers.
3. The miracles did not take place during a church meeting.
4. Men performed the miracles without enduring hours of agonizing prayer or by commanding God.
5. The miracles were performed by men not by prayer or commanding God.
6. The miracles were clear and seen by many.
7. The effectiveness of the miracle was not dependent upon the faith of the recipient.
8. There were no miracle failures.

Aside from the clear differences between apostolic miracles and the miracles of today, there is another vital element in the book of Acts which indicates the apostolic church was unique and is not to be the normative example. We can term this the issue of negative miracles. A prime example of a negative miracle involved Ananias and Sapphira, who dropped dead on command after lying to the Holy Spirit and the church (Acts 5:1-10). Similarly, a magician named Elymas opposed the apostles and was immediately blinded by Paul (Acts 13:11). Stories like this abound, clarifying that the first few years of apostolic ministry are a far cry from the normative church age experience. Any position which claims miracles still exist must not only show evidence of miracles, but also attest to the very difficult measures of church discipline. Clearly, these were acts done by apostolic authority and not by simple prayers of a faithful congregation.

In conclusion, the Book of Acts describes a unique beginning to the church age, where apostles wielded miraculous authority and thousands of unbelievers came to faith. However, these passages describe God's fulfillment of a prophetic promise that does not need to be fulfilled again in the church today. The sign-miracles confirming Old Testament prophecy and the resurrection of Jesus were limited to that period which marked the birth of the church and consisted of miracles far greater than anything imagined by modern mystic-miracle wonder-working movements of today.

Miraculous answers to prayer—by God—are not proof that individuals have the gift of miracles or healing. Further, since miraculous experiences may not be from God (Matt 7:22-23), all experiences must be verified by Scripture. Until adequate biblical support for today's supposed miracle claims are presented, there is no reason to give any credence to the leader or the practice.

There are many who say, "We need to be a first century church." If this is true, then I submit we need to study the example of the first century church rather than the first century apostles. The early churches seem to have been much like the average Bible-believing churches of today . . . They had problems with adultery, theft, heartless affection, factions, doctrine, etc. There's no basis for the belief that healers and other miracle workers were in the local churches at all. There is no evidence, as is so often naively assumed, that the New Testament churches were "turning the world upside down." It was Paul who was doing this! In fact, only a few churches were ever commended for their belief and behavior—Revelation 2 and 3 give us a realistic evaluation of the first century church. Of the seven churches, only two are spiritual and they are not characterized by miracle power.[3] So now,

---

[3] Edgar, *Miraculous Gifts*, 103.

with this context established for miracles, let's address the false-teaching that every believer should speak in tongues.

Speaking in Tongues

For the past 100 years the various charismata groups have proposed that speaking in tongues is a necessary sign of post-conversion baptism in the Spirit. However, adherents are not agreed on what actually constitutes speaking in tongues. Some say it's the ability to speak a foreign lan-guage, while others say that it is a prayer language. Sadly, this tangle has led to much confusion and insecurity around the world.

Adding to the confusion is the lack of support from church history. While the Third Wave/NAR camp claims to trace its lineage back to the first century church, this claim is, at best, misleading. As MacArthur writes:

> The historians and theologians of the early church unanimously maintained that tongues ceased to exist after the time of the apostles. The only exception of which we know was within the movement led by Montanus, a second century heretic who believed that divine revelation continued through him beyond the New Testament.
>
> Apparently no other tongues-speaking was practiced in Christianity until the seventeenth and eighteenth centuries, when it appeared in several Roman Catholic groups in Europe (Cevenols and Jansenists) and among the Shakers in New England. The nineteenth century Irvingites of London were marked by unbiblical claims of revelations and by "tongues-speak." For over 1,800 years the gift of tongues, along with the other miracle gifts, was unknown in the life and doctrine of orthodox Christianity.[4]

Montanus was a false prophet and never claimed the gift of tongues, Irenaeus referred to known languages not ecstatic speech, the Cevenols used children to prophesy and they wrongly predicted the return of Christ, the Irvingites led people into false doctrine, the Shakers weren't even Christian, and the Ranters were outright immoral, and none pro-

---

[4] John MacArthur, *1 Corinthians*, MacArthur New Testament Commentary (Chicago: Moody Press, 1984), 361.

fessed (the 20th century doctrine) that speaking in tongues is the sign of spirit baptism or the mark of a true Christian.

Tongues in the Greek Language

Understanding the definition of *glossa, the* Greek word for "tongue" is foundational in determining the course and function of biblical tongues. Language scholars Liddell and Scott write that biblical Greek held the term *glossa* to refer to "the tongue, organ of speech, or language (known or foreign)."[5] Renowned Greek scholars Moulton and Milligan confirm that biblical and secular Greek used *glossa* to mean "normal human language, local peculiarities of speech, or the physical tongue."[6] Additionally, Bible scholar Robert Gundry confirms that "the Greek Old Testament [Septuagint] always used the word *glossa* to reference human language, and sometimes of a nation in the sense of a language unit. *Glossa* occurs 114 times in the canonical books and never means unintelligible speech. It always refers to the tongue itself or speech."[7]

The clear position of scholars is that all biblical tongues refer to a language and not some form of ecstatic speech or unintelligible groaning, etc. Remarkably, the same can be true of classical Greek. Aristotle writes, "An ordinary word is one used by everybody, a *rare word* one used by some . . ."[8] [italics mine]. In classical Greek, the word *glotta* is the word translated "rare" in Aristotle's passage. *Glotta* (the Attic for *glossa*) does not describe a strange, obscure utterance but normal language.[9]

---

[5] Henry George Liddell and Robert Scott, *Greek-English Lexicon* (Oxford: Clarendon Press, 1968), 353.

[6] James Hope Moulton and George Milligan, *Vocabulary of Greek Testament: Illustrated from the Papyri and Other Non-Literary Sources* (London: Hodder and Stoughton, 1972), 128.

[7] Robert H. Gundry, "Ecstatic Utterance (N.E.B.)," *Journal of Theological Studies* 17, no. 2 (October 1966): 299.

[8] Aristotle, *Poetics* 1457b, accessed December 13, 2017, http://www.perseus.tufts.edu/hopper/text?doc=Perseus:abo:tlg,0086,034:1457b:2

[9] Johannes Behm, "*Glossa*," in *Theological Dictionary of the New Testament*, ed. Gerhard Kittel, ed. and trans. Geoffrey W. Bromiley (Grand Rapids, MI: Wm. B. Eerdmans, 1964), 1:719–726.

The ancient Greek biographer Plutarch agrees, "There is no occasion to be surprised at the revamping of *these words* into Greek . . . those who speak of *such word* [italics mine] as strange or unusual falsely accuse it of using barbarisms."[10] Note, Plutarch even provides contextual structure, clarifying why other words are merely foreign language and should not count people as barbarians. Clearly, the term *glotta* is used to describe Greek words which the ancient poets were attempting to revive.

The ancient Greek language, whether classical or biblical, didn't use *glossa* to mean ecstatic speech. In fact, time and again we see that this word translated in modern Bibles as "tongues" simply means a physical organ or a known language. This is foundational to the remainder of our discussion, proving that the Bible never commends ecstatic outbursts, mumbling, or private prayer languages.

Tongues in the Book of Acts

The New Testament uses the typical word for tongues 50 times. All of the passages are clear and undisputed except those describing the gift of tongues. This, however, was never meant to be confusing: The basic rule of interpretation is that passages must be interpreted by their most common usage unless the context clearly dictates otherwise.

There is little argument that the tongues spoken on the day of Pentecost in Acts refers to normal, foreign languages. Acts 2:4-8 states:

And they were all filled with the Holy Spirit and began to speak with other tongues, as the Spirit was giving them utterance. Now there were Jews living in Jerusalem, devout men from every nation under heaven. And when this sound occurred, the crowd came together, and were bewildered because each one of them was hearing them speak in his *own language*. They were amazed and astonished, saying, "Why, are not all these who are speaking Galileans? And how is it that we each hear them in our *own language* to which we were born?" [italics mine]

---

[10] Plutarch, *De Iside et Osiride 61*, accessed December 13, 2017, http://www.perseus.tufts.edu/hopper/text?doc=Perseus%3Atext%3A2008.01.0239%3A section%3D61.

The speaking described in this passage uses the words *glossa* and *dialektos*, meaning the language of the nation. Quite obviously the gift of tongues given to the apostles was so that they could preach to foreigners in the languages that they could understand. This is the only passage in the entire Bible that directly describes the gift of tongues given by the Holy Spirit. Given its clarity, this passage must be used to determine the meaning of any other passages on tongues we find unclear. Anyone claiming a different doctrine of tongues would need strong evidence that depicts tongues as something different from its seminal biblical depiction and clear instruction.

The two other mentions of tongues in Acts happened in a manner similar to Acts 2. Specifically, they came quickly and were used as an evangelistic language, leading foreigners to understand the Gospel (Acts 10:46; 19:6). They both had the same characteristics: (1) the phenomena came suddenly (like at Pentecost), apart from any seeking; (2) in a calm and orderly way; and, (3) in a missionary environment. There were no trances, no emotive outbursts, and the amazement is always on the part of the unsaved hearers and not the evangelist. There is no depiction of jerking, quaking, convulsions, barking, dancing, or drunken behavior.

Tongues in 1 Corinthians

1 Corinthians 12–14 is often cited as the foundation for speaking in tongues. It is the longest portion of the Bible devoted to tongues, but interestingly the passage doesn't fully define the word "tongues." The argument made for tongues as a signature sign of the Holy Spirit's filling is that the tongues spoken of in this chapter are a form of "ecstatic language," "angel speak," or "prayer language." Various portions of these chapters are used to promote this position, but each of them are contextually, historically, and experientially inaccurate. Let's consider the most widely argued texts that are in support of tongues as an ecstatic utterance.

Tongues of Angels in 1 Corinthians 13

Many suggest that 1 Corinthians 13:1 references the tongues of angels, "If I speak with the tongues of men and of angels, but do not have love, I have become a noisy gong. . . ." However, a broader reading of the text indicates that Paul is using hyperbole. Notice the three examples he uses in this rhetorical piece; Paul's answers have been added in brackets.

> If I speak with the tongues of men [which I can do] and of angels [which I cannot do], but do not have love, I have become a noisy gong or a clanging cymbal. If I have the gift of prophecy [which I can do], and know all mysteries and all knowledge and if I have all faith so as to remove mountains [which I cannot do], but do not have love, I am nothing. And if I give all my possessions to feed the poor [which I can do], and if I surrender my body to be burned [which I cannot do], but do not have love, it profits me nothing.[11]

As you can see, Paul is setting up a series of hypothetical exaggerations explaining what he can and cannot do; indicating that all of it is useless without love. One of the things he cannot do is speak with angels. Further evidence undermining the charismatic interpretation of tongues as an angelic language can be found in 1 Corinthians 13:8 which says tongues will one day cease. Obviously angelic language doesn't need to cease. So why would tongues cease if they were an angelic language? Still further evidence rests in the many biblical depictions of angels speaking to men. Why would men need to speak an angelic language when angels can clearly understand human language? This text in no way describes an ecstatic utterance or angelic language.

Prayer Languages in 1 Corinthians 14

The modern charismatic movement derives most of its defense for prayer language or ecstatic speech from the text of 1 Corinthians 14. As shown above, there is every reason—grammatically, culturally, and historically—to interpret this passage just like it's Acts 2's counterpart—referencing tongues (*glossa*) as a language spoken by men through the power of the Holy Spirit.

It is important to remember the following: (1) There is no evidence for the word tongue (*glossa*) being used to mean unintelligible speech. (2) There is no evidence in the Old Testament of people practicing this speech. (3) *Glossa* means foreign language in every other

---

[11] "Surrender" references a hand-over *without* reason (hyperbolic sarcasm), clearly not something Paul would do or recommend.

part of the New Testament. And, (4) Acts 2 is the only clear description of tongues as a gift, which clearly means a foreign language.

There are seven points to consider about 1 Corinthians 14 which proves that Paul is describing a foreign tongue and not an ecstatic utterance.

What is the context?

First, 1 Corinthians 14 is set in the context of an assembly (church gathering). This is important to recognize because Paul is not writing to individuals about their private prayer life. The context refers to a situation where others are present, where an interpreter may or not be around, and where others will want to speak and join in. Notice the key terms in 1 Corinthians 14: "edifies the church" (v. 4), "edified" (v. 5), "assembly" (v. 12), "in the assembly" (v. 19), "gathered together" (v. 23), "keep silent" (v. 28), and "women silent in assemblies" (v. 34). Thus, the overarching theme of 1 Corinthians 14 is that the assembly needs to be edified in such a way that all can enjoy (the teaching) and in a way that is far superior to signs, which unbelievers can't understand. The overarching theme of 1 Corinthians 14 isn't in support of tongues but to limit tongues. As Gundry states,

> Paul's is stating that the tongue is unintelligible not because it's an ecstatic language, but because neither the speaker nor anyone else in the congregation happens to have the gift of interpretation. . . . It is the absence of interpretation which makes the tongue unintelligible.[12]

Obviously the Corinthians were confused in their worship services, not because people are babbling, but because people were speaking human languages unknown to them and there was no one there to interpret. Paul commands them to rectify this situation.

What are the mysteries?

Second, many focus in on the word "mysteries" (1 Cor 14:2), implying that a private prayer language connects them to quasi-spiritual mysteries. However, the term "mysteries" is a common biblical term for "something not formerly understood" (Matt 13:11; Eph 1:9; 5:32; Col 2:2; 1 Tim 3:9) and simply means spiritual truth new to the age in

---

[12] Gundry, "Ecstatic Utterance," 302–303.

which a person lives. For example, the arrival of Jesus was a mystery revealed, the second advent of Jesus is a mystery yet to be revealed, etc. This in no way infers that believers are to be seeking mystical experiences.

Why does Paul refer to instruments?

Third, 1 Corinthians 14:7-9 says,

> Yet *even* lifeless things, either flute or harp, in producing a sound, if they do not produce a distinction in the tones, how will it be known what is played on the flute or on the harp? For if the bugle produces an indistinct sound, who will prepare himself for battle? So also you, unless you utter by the tongue speech that is clear, how will it be known what is spoken? For you will be speaking into the air.

These verses illustrate Paul's primary focus—speech which if not understood is useless. The emphasis here isn't on the indistinct sounds but on the failure of the sounds to communicate. Paul is saying that if a bugle blurts out a bunch of noise which isn't in a musical form, no one will understand or enjoy the sound. The same was true when many Corinthians stood up and spoke in various languages without interpretation—no one was strengthened, no one was encouraged, and unbelievers weren't reached.

What is barbarian speech?

Fourth, 1 Corinthians 14:11 states, "Therefore if I do not know the meaning of the voice I shall be a barbarian to the one speaking. . . ." The term *barbaros* was a well-understood phrase in Greek culture meaning "one who speaks a strange language." In fact, the four times it's used in the New Testament, it refers to non-Greeks or those of a different culture who speak a different language. It's simply a term that references non-Greek people who sounded different due to their ethnicity and language barrier.

Why does Paul refer to signs?

Fifth, in 1 Corinthians 14:20-22 Paul uses the Old Testament to support his instruction that these other languages were an evangelistic outreach to outsiders, not meant as personal prayer languages for personal edification. Paul writes:

Brethren, do not be children in your thinking; yet in evil be infants, but in your thinking be mature. In the Law it is written, "BY MEN OF STRANGE TONGUES AND BY THE LIPS OF STRANGERS I WILL SPEAK TO THIS PEOPLE, AND EVEN SO THEY WILL NOT LISTEN TO ME," says the Lord. So then tongues are for a sign, not to those who believe but to unbelievers; but prophecy *is for a sign*, not to unbelievers but to those who believe. . . ." (1 Cor 14:20–22)

Paul quotes Isaiah 28:11, where the Hebrew refers to men stammering in speech. The word "stammering" (*la'ag*) means "mocking" or "deriding."[13] The context speaks of God's judgment upon Israel by a nation (the Assyrians) which speaks a language foreign to their ears. In 1 Corinthians 14:22, Paul uses the Greek word *hoste* (so then) to connect the quote with v. 21, introducing a conclusion based on the preceding statement. Because verse 21 is a quote regarding other languages, the conclusion in verse 22 must also refer to language. Paul would not build a direct argument regarding magical prayer languages or unintelligible utterances on a passage referring to normal language in the Old Testament.

Why does Paul mention private prayer?

Sixth, in 1 Corinthians 14:28 Paul corrects the person who's been doing the speaking out of turn and causing confusion: "if there be no interpreter, let him keep quiet in the assembly, and speak to himself and to God." Some falsely interpret this direction as referring to prayer language when in fact it's a call for order: "If you can't do things in order then sit down and keep it to yourself!" Paul in this context clearly wants people to stop distracting the assembly with their outbursts.

Why does Paul set an order?

Seventh, 1 Corinthians 14:32–33 sets the rules for prophecy—and implicitly the same argument would apply to those speaking in tongues. Paul expects the church services to be held and conducted with order, with only one person speaking at a time, and that the women are to stay silent. Notice, this verse says nothing about the style of speech, only about the direction and control of the speech. There is nothing

---

[13] Francis Brown, S. R. Driver, and Charles Briggs, "לָעַג [la'ag]" in *Brown Driver Briggs Hebrew and English Lexicon* (Oxford, UK: Clarendon, 1907), 4922, Bible-Works.

here to indicate tongues as anything other than a foreign language spoken for the good of unbelievers.

There is nothing in 1 Corinthians 12-14 which requires a special meaning for tongues contrary to the historically documented meaning of Acts 2's *glossa*. In fact, the idea of an Acts 2 non-understood foreign language is acceptable in every instance, and the only form which is appropriate. The evidence shows that both Acts 2 and 1 Corinthians 12-14 reference a non-learned language spoken by the early Christians. This stands in opposition to the idea of an ecstatic utterance made in church or as a private prayer language at home for three principle reasons:

1. The evidence for ecstatic speech is mere inference.
2. Ecstatic speech is contrary to the purpose of biblical tongues.
3. Ecstatic speech is contrary to the purpose of biblical gifts (evangelism).

Anglican Archbishop and scholar Peter Jensen once traced the writings of the early church fathers on this issue, noting their position on tongues, and concluded that by and large tongues were always held as a human language. In his article in *Evangelical Quarterly*, Jensen reviews the teaching of Aquinas and Augustine on this topic:

> In an earlier period, Aquinas discusses glossolalia, or "the grace of tongues" in the Summa Theologica. He conducts this discussion on the assumption that "tongues" constitute a miraculous but intelligible phenomenon, in which the speaker is able to preach in a foreign language: . . . both Paul and the other apostles were divinely instructed in the languages of all the nations sufficiently for the requirements of teaching the faith. In this, Aquinas quotes Augustine to the same effect; a quotation which includes the further thought that this miracle had ceased: 'Whereas even now the Holy Ghost is received, yet no-one speaks in the tongues of all nations, because the Church herself already speaks the languages of all nations: since whoever is not in the Church receives not the Holy Ghost.' That foreign languages (rather than ecstatic babble) is meant seems to have been the position of most of the Fathers.[14]

---

[14] Peter F. Jensen, "Calvin, Charismatics and Miracles," *Evangelical Quarterly* 51, no. 3 (1979), 131-144.

To review:
- 1 Corinthians 13:1 references tongues of men as a language.
- 1 Corinthians 14 is set in the context of an orderly public service where people are learning the newly revealed "mysteries" of Christ Jesus (14:2).
- They are commanded to speak with a goal of encouraging people (1 Cor 14:7-9).
- The languages were foreign (1 Cor 14:11).
- These languages were specifically for the unbelievers who were new to the church (1 Cor 14:21-23).
- These speaking in foreign languages must be done in an orderly way (1 Cor 14:27).
- And if one couldn't do this then this person was instructed to sit down and keep it to themselves (1 Cor 14:28).

Conclusion

Based on all we've studied, can we confidently report that the gift of tongues has ceased as 1 Corinthians 13:8 said it would? Has the gift to wield miracles ceased? The answer is a resounding yes. One incontro-vertible fact explains why—the gift of New Testament apostleship has ceased. The gift was clearly temporary, given to specific men, ending with one specific man (Paul), with an apostolic gifting that was promised to fade, and that the normative experience of all Christian orthodoxy is in support of this fact for over 1,800 years, proves overwhelmingly that this is what the Holy Spirit intended.

Ephesians 2:20 clarifies that the apostles were the foundation. 2 Corinthians 12:12 explains that the apostles were given ability to perform special signs, so clearly if the apostles are gone there is no one left to perform the sign miracles at will.

Appendix 4

The Myth of Being Slain in the Spirit

Introduction

Mystic-miracles workers claim that the truth of their message is verified when people are slain in the spirit. Here is an illustration of what so many young people are experiencing today:

It had been over three hours since the service started, and I was really starting to feel God's presence in the building. As I stood next to my friend, the music was deep and intense. The lighting made everything feel so intimate, and a slight fog danced through the air. The lead singer's voice was so beautiful—Jesus Culture's music is so anointed. The voices all around me sang in unison, and I felt myself slipping into a deep, rhythmic trance as I swayed to the song. The pastor had been continuously telling us to expect an encounter with God and that God was going to touch us all in some special way. Could this be the solution to my problems in life? I'd been through so much heart-ache and insecurity. I was tired of being told that God's word and prayer was enough. Maybe this was the real deal—maybe this was the encounter I needed. Just then, the pastor interrupted the singing and shouted, "Jesus is here! The anointing is yours! If you want a fresh touch from God get down here to the front of the stage!" I looked at my friend quickly and said, "Are you coming?! This is it!" He shrugged nervously and stayed put. I think he was skeptical of this sort of thing—he's a Baptist. Oh well, I thought—his loss. Bodies poured out into the aisles as people just like me hurried desperately down to the stage. As I got closer to the front I felt adrenaline pump through my veins and soon found a spot just a few feet away from the pastor. Looking up at him I felt like God was telling him who to lay hands on. His eyes scanned the sea of young people below his platform. Then, my moment came. He told one of his assistants, "Get that girl right there! The power of God is all over her!" I felt so special that he picked me it caused me to sob uncontrollably. I was pulled up on the platform and it felt like I had made it to the holy of holies. My hands were shaking from the nerves, my breaths were short but heavy, and I sensed the catchers getting into place. Then he shouted, "FIRE!!! on you..." The emotion of the moment was too much for me to take as I felt something take a hold of my body. I abandoned all rationale and was powerfully forced to the ground. My body began to convulse and contort while I was laying on the stage; sounds poured out of my mouth I'd never made before. I could hear and feel other bodies beginning to fall around me and on me. Some people were laughing hysterically, others touched me and groaned deeply, and some were screaming while crawling on all fours. I have heard some Christians say this sort of experience was demonic, while others say it's just hypnosis. To be honest, I haven't seen it in the Bible and don't really know what it is . . . but I really feel like it's the Holy Spirit.

This is just a glimpse into what is taking place all over the world through the eyes of someone who claims to be slain in the spirit. Over 500 million charismatics and 1.5 billion Hindus in the Kundalini Awakening practice slaying people in the spirit; so it is no exaggeration to state that at least 2/7 of the world's population has beliefs that are tied to falling or shaking under the power of some sort of spirit. With this significant representation of the population, being slain the spirit is not a fringe behavior; it is now mainstream spiritualism and considered highly normative—it's everywhere. Consequently, many Christians are scared to death of their children ever going to one of these services, but when asked what the issue really is, most cannot explain but to say that "it's unbiblical" or "not God." We need a better answer.

In the Christian-charismatic world, what exactly does someone mean when they say, "I got slain in the spirit!"? This phrase describes what many believe to be a touch from God that overtakes a person's motor-control and sends their body falling to the ground—sometimes stiff and lifeless and other times writhing and flopping around. Those who ardently defend this practice claim that it's God's manifest presence in a service that causes people to fall over. According to them, God's power is usually imparted by a pastor who lays his hands on them, blows his breath on them, waves his hand, waves his jacket, or shouts a phrase like "Fire!" or "Touch!" These gestures cause people to go flying in all directions. Sometimes it even occurs when a certain song is sung by the worship band or because people are overcome with emotion during a portion of the service. Often times those being slain in the spirit will be seen on the ground making animal sounds, crawling, shaking, convulsing, weeping, laughing, and experiencing trance-like euphoria.[1] Some say they feel electricity when the pastor touches them, others feel warmth, while others are not able to stand under their own strength for hours afterwards. All of this is believed to be the work of the Holy Spirit as He refreshes and renews spiritually empty and broken people.

What biblical evidence is there to support the belief that the Holy Spirit is causing people to shake, shout, laugh, bark, crawl, or convulse in the church? When God interacts with people in the Bible, does He electrocute them or lead them into a seemingly drunken state where speech is slurred and the body moved uncontrolled? Can a preacher shouting "Fire!" really cause heaven to invade your life on earth? Or, is it possible that some of these charismatic experiences are identical to the demonic manifestations of "being slain" that are found in Hinduism? The best way to understand the charismatic practice of being slain in the spirit is to understand the position of those who support and practice it.

What do 'Slain in the Spirit' Enthusiasts Claim?

First, there are a number of varying claims depending on what charismatic group is explaining them. That, in and of itself, proves how much confusion there is surrounding the practice. Here are several key claims:

- Slain in the spirit experiences are the result of the manifest presence of God the Father.

---

[1] "Heidi Baker - Demonic Impartation," posted October 9, 2014, accessed February 1, 2018, https://youtu.be/16H84rcaqyk?t=3m19s. Heidi Baker causes a young boy to roar like an animal, crawl, and convulse on the ground like he's on a string.

- Jesus is the one doing the slaying.
- The Holy Spirit is a force that cannot be stopped. When He touches people they fall.
- People who are empty need to be slain in the spirit to get filled with the Spirit.
- When God touches human flesh, something will happen.
- When heaven touches earth, things shake.
- The power of God is overwhelming. When it shows up, people fall.

To support these general claims, charismatic enthusiasts use specific Bible passages as proof texts for being slain in the spirit. Christians who aren't biblically literate won't usually notice the interpretive gymnastics being utilized, but when we study what the Bible actually says, the myths behind being slain in the spirit get biblically busted.

Myth #1: It Happened in the Old Testament

"It happened that when the priests came from the holy place, the cloud filled the house of the Lord, so that the priests could not stand to minister because of the cloud, for the glory of the Lord filled the house of the Lord." (1 Kings 8:10-11)

The context of this passage is the completion of Solomon's temple into which the glory of God descended upon the temple to signify His sovereignty over the nation of Israel. The priests, overwhelmed by God's glory, could not to stand to minister (1 Kings 8:10; 2 Chron 5:13). We see something similar with Moses when he was unable to enter the tent of meeting because of the cloud of glory that filled it (Ex 40:34-38). But in neither case is there any indication that these men were knocked down by God's presence. We are told the priests could not stand, but this does not mean they fell down. We see many instances in the Old Testament where people "fell on their faces" (Num 20:6; 1 Chron 29:20; Gen 17:3; Lev 9:24; Num 24:4; 1 Kings 18:39; Neh 8:6). Yet these cases are always when the person is bowing in profound respect and awe of God's wonder.[2] So given this context, it seems reasonable to suggest that our priests in 1 Kings may have

---

[2] Mark F. Rooker, *Leviticus*, The New American Commentary 3A (Nashville, TN: Broadman & Holman, 2000), 155.

simply bowed down in worship. Outside of the efforts of modern faith-healers attempting to justify their experience, nothing in the passage itself comes close to describing today's practice of slaying in the spirit.

If charismatic enthusiasts insist on using these passages as justification for their behavior, then they must resolve the problem of how the Old Testament priests were unable to stand in the presence of the Lord; meanwhile, modern day preachers, catchers, organ players, singers, and rest of the audience are able to stand, clap, use the restrooms, and film the experience with their cell phones for YouTube. If the glory of God has filled the room, why are some people immune? Are we truly to be-lieve that a few select men like Todd White or Benny Hinn are able to control the glory of God?

There are a few other scattered verses that receive a similarly twisted interpretative treatment:

- Abram fell into a deep sleep (Gen 15:12).
- Mount Sinai shakes from the presence of the Lord (Ex 19:18).
- The Spirit of the Lord came mightily upon David (1 Sam 16:13).
- The Spirit of the Lord came upon Gideon (Judg 6:34).

There is not an honest theologian on earth who can make any of these verses truly mean that being slain in the spirit is biblical. Did God move in powerful ways throughout the Bible and does He still today? Absolutely. Is there a single instance in the Old Testament where He "slays someone in the spirit" or instructs a prophet to form a fire tunnel and knock people down in a heaping pile?[3] Absolutely not.

---

[3] "Bethel Redding Fire Tunnel with Puppets," posted February 21, 2016, accessed February 1, 2018, https://youtu.be/kY6AJOEWdcQ. This video shows a Bethel fire tunnel with manifestations and the use an actual puppet (not a typo) to lay hands on people. There is laughing, falling, odd human noises, puppet slapping, shaking, and convulsing. In a fire tunnel leaders and assigned ministers stand on two sides to form a long pathway down the middle. People walk down the gauntlet and are touched by everyone in order to get the "fire of God" on their life. See also, "Fire of The Holy Ghost tunnel JESUS Conf," posted December 17, 2015, accessed February 2, 2018, https://youtu.be/Wi60cOWVIXk.

Myth #2: It Happened in the New Testament

They answered Him, "Jesus the Nazarene." He said to them, "I am He." And Judas also, who was betraying Him, was standing with them. So when He said to them, "I am He," they drew back and fell to the ground. (John 18:5-6)

In this incident, Jesus, the Son of God, stood face to face with his betrayer and a "Roman cohort [soldiers], officers of the chief priests, and the Pharisees." With a simple declaration of his identity, Jesus caused these wicked men to fall to the ground. This ultimate sign of power and authority by Christ was a clear display of His divine sovereignty over those He would soon allow to hang him on the cross. Not once was the Lamb of God not fully God and not once was He without control.

When we observe these men falling to the ground before Jesus at His spoken word, several things cannot be overlooked: (1) They were His enemies. (2) He did not impart His anointing to them; (3) They did not have a euphoric encounter with God. (4) They did not manifest his glory by barking, shaking, convulsing, or sobbing. (5) They were not filled with the Spirit. (6) They were not healed while lying on the ground. And, (7) They carried on with arresting Him. The events of this passage cannot be divorced from the application of this text. What Jesus did and how the mob responded offers no support for modern day practices.

There are other New Testament verses that receive a similarly twisted interpretative treatment:

- Peter and John lay hands on people who receive the Holy Spirit (Acts 8:17).
- Handkerchiefs that touched Paul were used to heal and deliver people (Acts 19:12).
- Paul was knocked off his horse by a beam of light (Acts 9:3-4; 22:6-7).
- John falls on his face before Jesus out of fear. Jesus says, "Do not be afraid" (Rev 1:17).

To use any of these New Testament examples of God's power as support for today's aberrant practice of slaying people in the spirit is an unbiblical position based on a dangerously self-serving interpretation.

There is nothing in the Bible that supports the practice of slaying people in the spirit or being slain in the spirit, nor does it even use those terms. Some may argue that the term "Trinity" is not in the Bible either and yet we believe in the Trinity. This line of argumentation is invalid because the doctrine of the Trinity has been established through countless passages that describe the persons of the Father, Son, and Holy Spirit—and we apply it exactly as Scripture teaches it. Terminology is not the issue when determining the biblical evidence for being slain in the spirit—finding any evidence is. The burden of proof is on the mystic-miracle workers seeking to justify their theology through practices which more closely resemble the demonic not Scripture.

What Happens When People Are 'Slain in the Spirit'?

Since we conclude that being slain in the spirit is not found in the Bible, there must be other factors at work. After 26 years of personally experiencing or being a part of tens of thousands of slayings, I [Costi] have made it a habit of placing all of that experience under the filter of Scripture. In doing so, I've come to the conclusion that there are five reasonable explanations for why people fall under the spell of being slain in the spirit.

Reason #1: Peer Pressure

Peer pressure at these sort of services is intense. Nobody wants to look bad or make the preacher look bad. It is widely believed that there is something wrong with you if you don't feel God's presence and have a manifestation of some sort, so peer pressure plays a huge factor in falling. Sadly, kids end up being the biggest loser in this forced behavior as they seek to please and soon are brainwashed into the system. In many cases, people see others falling and just follow suit. Finally, it is common for seekers who come to these services to think they have to fall down in order to get the experience that the preacher is promising.

Reason #2: The Power of Suggestion

The power of suggestion, like we see in hypnosis, is real. Documentaries like *Miracles for Sale* have proven that the power of suggestion and hypnosis can be used to make complete strangers do whatever the hypnotist commands.[4] This isn't news to those with an understanding of psychology and social science, but many Christians are still unaware that many charismatic extremists who slay people in the spirit are experts at hypnotic suggestion and psychological manipulation. Three hours of sensual and soothing music, countless bursts of saying, "Jesus is here! He is going to touch you! You are going to feel something you've never felt before! Just receive it!" gets people in the mood. Then, they are ripe for manipulation.

Reason #3: People Want to Fall Down

Reverence is a big deal in Third Wave, NAR, and charismatic extremist circles. People are taught to honor leaders in a god-like fashion because they are viewed as God's exclusively anointed, divine representatives on earth. Many former followers of these movements have admitted that they wanted a deeper connection with God and wanted the anointing that was being promised by the leader—so they chose to fall in hopes of having a spiritual experience. This often leads to the weeping, praying, and emotional responses seen after the pastor lays his hands on them.

Reason #4: People Are Faking It

I [Costi] have personally interacted with friends, family, and followers who have faked it. By the grace of God people who don't grow up in charismatic chaos like I have don't have any idea this happens. But when you grow up with a special anointing service every week and it lasts 4 hours at a time—you start falling just to get it over with. I once asked someone close to me why they threw themselves back and acted so crazy on the platform, to which he explained, "Come on man, we gotta make him look good and get this over with." Make no mistake about it—people fake it.

Reason #5: Being Slain in the Spirit is Demonic

In many cases where a false teacher is involved, modern day slayings in the spirit are akin to biblical accounts of someone who is experiencing demonic influence or possession (Mark 9:17–18). This is

---

[4] Derren Brown, "Miracles for Sale," posted April 28, 2011, accessed December 13, 2017, https://youtu.be/iuP5uOI7Xwc.

not meant to be a blanket statement that all slaying in the spirit practices today are strictly demonic, but when the other four reasons aren't in play, you can bet it's not some innocent charismatic behavior. Some may wonder how anyone could dare attribute this to demonic behavior, but think about this for a second: Can a false teacher, teaching a false gospel, and being used by Satan (2 Cor 11:13–15), lay hands on a person seeking God and cause them to experience the true Holy Spirit? No. Spiritual beings are real and their powers in this world are real. Now, demonic powers cannot compete with God's power, but when a person opens himself or herself up to demonic influence, should we be surprised that the devil takes advantage of that opportunity?

At best, well-meaning people are seeking an encounter with God in the wrong way through the wrong means and will end up confused and disappointed. At worst, desperate people and apostates are being overtaken by hypnosis, the power of suggestion, demonic forces, or a false spirit that they believe to be the Holy Spirit.

If it doesn't match the Bible, isn't found in the Bible, or can't be truly backed up by proper interpretation of the Bible, you're not missing out on anything. The Holy Spirit is accessible today through the power of the Gospel, and He exists to glorify the Lord Jesus Christ, not to put on a His own show (John 16:14–15). If people surrender to Christ, embrace the true work of the Spirit in their life, and submit to the Bible as sufficient and final revelation, being slain in the spirit becomes irrelevant. No matter what a person's position is on spiritual gifts today, all discerning Christians can confidently say, "I'll pass" when it comes to being slain in the spirit.

Appendix 5

Can You Be Healed by a False Teacher?

A few years ago an excited woman in her 20's ran up to me [Costi] one Sunday at church—she was a newer attendee who had been kicking the tires on our church for a few weeks when my last name must have clicked. It's not like we talk about it every Sunday at Mission Bible—our members don't really care. We have a lot of important ministry to do and I'm just another one of the pastors. But sometimes it comes out in conversations and you never know what you're going to get. An angry ex-faith-healer-enthusiast who threatens a shake down if I don't pay them back what my uncle stole from them? An excited believer who came out of the jaws of deception like me? It's hit or miss.

This particular Sunday it was a little more complicated. Here's a paraphrase of what she exclaimed just outside the sanctuary doors:

> Costi Hinn? Like as in Benny Hinn? Oh my goodness! Your uncle is part of my testimony. He totally healed me of scoliosis [curved spine]. It was late one night when I was watching his program, *This is Your Day*, and he told everyone who is sick or in pain put their hands on the TV up against his hands and believe for a miracle. I did. Then, I felt this warmth go up my spine and I just knew I was healed! After that experience, my spine got better and I stand here today completely healed with a straightened spine. I know you don't agree with all that he teaches but he's a part of my story and God used him to heal me. I'll always be grateful for your uncle.

This is familiar ground for a lot of pastors and Christians who are approached often by people who claim that God is doing great things through a false teacher and/or that God used a false teacher to heal them. Some of these claims are made even by well-meaning, genuinely converted Christians who no longer follow the false teacher but are adamant that God used the false teacher to heal them or provide them with some particularly meaningful mystical experience. I'm reminded of one of my favorite R. C. Sproul quotes:

> The truth of a teacher's words is determined not by the feats he can perform but by the orthodoxy of what he teaches. We are never to follow anyone who perverts the truth of God's Word, no matter how gifted that person is, how large of an organization that person commands, or how amazing that person's work seems to be.[1]

So, is there any credence to a claim of miraculous healing at the hands of a false teaching faith healer? How should a pastor or leader handle such claims when there is clearly a danger in making any kind of endorsement of a false teacher? For our purposes here, let's look at four potential responses (or scenarios) that can be useful in helping people understand what they may (or may not) have experienced.

Response #1: You were mercifully healed by God; and He mercifully snatched you from a wolf.

This particular response would be applicable if an individual proved to be a true believer, was verifiably healed, and had been saved from following a false teacher's ministry out of ignorance. Since God is still a healer, it is certainly possible that He has healed this individual, but the biblical standard for healing must still apply.

First, throughout Scripture we see divine healing at the hands of God as: (1) immediate, (2) unquestionable, (3) irreversible, (4) not dependent on special healing services, (5) not solely dependent on faith, (6) much more than curing a cold, (7) accompanying a call to flee from sin, (8) not dependent on continuous confessions, (9) not solely dependent on proximity, and (10) possible through prayer.

One could certainly add to this list but if, generally speaking, the healing matches the biblical standard, then praise God! God heals in many different ways, but false teachers are not able to duplicate the divine power it takes to match God's criteria. Even if in the slightest way, they will fall short.

Second, throughout Scripture we see that true believers cannot and will not stay deceived, so even if someone appears to be have been

---

[1] "False Signs and Wonders," Ligonier Ministries, accessed January 9, 2018, https://www.ligonier.org/learn/devotionals/false-signs-and-wonders/.

healed, there may have been other powers at work if that individual has not come out from the clutches of false teachers. Sheep ultimately come to hear and follow the Shepherd's voice (John 10:27), saved people grow in Christ-likeness (Phil 1:6), children of God walk in the truth (1 John 3:18-19), and true disciples—though not always perfect—will pursue obedience to God's Word out of love for Christ (John 14:15).

Plainly, we can gather a short list of truths and offer these to genuinely saved people who have experienced healing, but mistakenly believe they were healed by a false teacher:

1. Give God the credit for healing you if it fits the biblical criteria.
2. Give God the credit for healing you through medical means if you've received treatment and were healed from it.
3. God is sovereign in healing, and in saving. He has mercifully done both in your life.
4. He spoke through a donkey (Num 22:28-30); turned a murderer into an Apostle (Acts 9); and healed a man's ear who was with Judas the Betrayer, the Roman soldiers, and the Jewish religious leaders when they came to arrest Jesus (Luke 22:49-51). He has graciously worked in your life in spite of your prior ignorance, blindly following false teachers.
5. Reject false teachers as agents of Satan (2 Cor 11:13-15), not as anointed vessels who "God uses despite some shortcomings."
6. Seek wise counsel for quantifying your testimony and explaining it biblically.

We hope you know someone who has been healed and would benefit from these truths and we encourage you to pass them along. It's likely, however, you will eventually meet someone that needs help, as described in one of the following responses.

Response #2: You were temporarily healed by the power of suggestion, hypnosis, or sleight of hand.

Wouldn't it be nice if our list could end with only one response to being healed by a false teacher? People, however, need to understand that if their healing, relief from pain, or euphoric experience was temporary, it was not cut short because of their own lack of faith or negative confession—it was because it was all part of the game. God healing does not allow people to relapse into a repetitive cycle of illness and healing. An honest discussion about failed healings is needed.

Studies have shown that the placebo effect is real, that hypnosis can cause people to do and feel things they'd otherwise never do or feel, and that the power of suggestion can cause people's bodies to respond in temporary ways—without the lasting results. This reality is nothing new. Back in the late 1980's, Dr. Normal Geisler's book, *Signs and Wonders*, shed light on a very confusing era in evangelicalism. The Charismatic Renewal era (approx. 1960-1983) had given way to what was being called "The Third Wave." The Third Wave was taking Charismatic practices to new mainstream heights and Geisler's book provided important answers. In his chapter, "Psychological or Supernatural," he quotes Dr. Paul Brand's original article in *Christianity Today* on the mind's power to control or even heal the body:

> In the placebo effect, faith in simple sugar pills stimulates the mind to control pain and even heal some disorders. In some experiments among those with terminal cancer, morphine was an effective painkiller in two-thirds of patients, but placebos were equally effective in half of those! The placebo tricks the mind into believing relief has come, and the body responds accordingly . . . In a false pregnancy, a woman believes so strongly in her pregnant condition that her mind directs an extraordinary sequence of activities: it increases hormone flow, enlarges breasts, suspends menstruation, induces morning sickness, and even prompts labor contractions.[2]

Geisler provides further evidence about the power of the mind:

> Dr. William Nolen explains that "the patient who suddenly discovers . . . that he can now move an arm or a leg that was previously paralyzed had that paralysis as a result of an emotional, not a physical disturbance." It is known that "neurotics and hysterics will frequently be relieved of their symptoms by the suggestions and min-

---

[2] Paul Brand and Philip Yancey, "A Surgeon's View Of Divine Healing," *Christianity Today* 27, no. 18 (November 1983): 19, quoted in Norman L Geisler, *Signs And Wonders* (Wheaton, IL: Tyndale House, 1988), 78-79.

istrations of charismatic healers. It is in treating patients of this sort that healers claim their most dramatic triumphs." So "there is nothing miraculous about these cures. Psychiatrists, internists, G.P.'s, any M.D. who does psychiatric therapy, relieve thousands of such patients of their symptoms every year." But they do it by purely natural means, claiming no special supernatural powers.[3]

Not only have many faithful Christian theologians put in hours of study to help us understand false faith healers in contrast to biblical truth, but even unbelievers have been able to shed light on the deception. In his 2011 documentary, *Miracles for Sale*, a world-renowned hypnotist and illusionist goes undercover in one of the most jaw-dropping exposes ever recorded. He trains a man who had no prior experience with hypnotism or faith-healing to be a faith-healer. Numerous modern faith-healers are little more than scam artists who use a false understanding of biblical truth to exploit the sick for monetary gain.

Unfortunately, many people—both Christians and non-Christians alike—have been duped by faith-healers who use hypnotic strategies and the power of suggestion to provide temporary relief from ailments. The real losers in this game of winner-take-all are the sick and hurting people who are left wondering what they've done to keep God from healing them completely.

Response #3: You've been deceived by a demonic, or counterfeit, sign.

This response isn't a popular one but the Word of God gives room for situations in which a power other than God is at work either to perform a legitimate sign or falsify one so well that it's uncritically believed. Here some examples from Scripture that provide undeniable evidence that satanic and demonic power is allowed under the sovereignty of God and legitimate to some degree—whether falsified or not:

1. Jesus doesn't refer to "false" signs and wonders when He tells miraculous workers that He never "knew" them (Matt 7:23). Those *could* be legitimate, demonic signs.

---

[3] William Nolen, *Healing: A Doctor in Search of a Miracle* (New York: Random House, 1974), 287, quoted in Geisler, *Signs And Wonders*, 79-80.

2. Jesus is also clear that in the last days "false Christs and false prophets will arise and will show great signs and wonders, so as to mislead, if possible, even the elect" (Matt 24:24; Mark 13:22).
3. Paul points out that the man of lawlessness will come in accordance with the activity of Satan, with "all power and signs and false wonders" (2 Thess 2:9).
4. Paul also assures that false prophets will disguise themselves as workers of righteousness (2 Cor 11:15).
5. The seven sons of Sceva were completely overpowered by evil spirits who "leaped on them" via a man they possessed (Acts 19:14-16).
6. Satan can bind people with sickness (Luke 13:16). If such an individual is converted, Satan and his oppressive force through disease would conceivably both be gone. In cases like these, salvation is primarily the miracle, the physical relief from satanic sickness is not—the person has simply gone back to his pre-possessed state of health.
7. Satan could stop Paul from going forward in his missionary plans (1 Thess 2:17-18).

Satan is the father of lies and has mastered the art of deception. It is very likely that many false teachers in the signs and wonders movement are "deceiving and being deceived" (2 Tim 3:13) by demonic means. Spiritual warfare is real.

Response #4: You are being used by darkness to deceive people.

There is one final response you may receive and it's probably the last one on the list for a reason—use it sparingly. Simply put, it's possible that a person is lying and being used to deceive others or is being deceived. They were never sick in the first place, or they had a minor ailment that was healed by their own body's self-healing capabilities (built by God) and they see it as a way to get attention. Similar to little children who make millions of dollars off of false stories about going to heaven, people claiming healing can make a lot of money off of books and films but offer zero theological value to evangelicalism. The accumulation of wealth is not proof of God's blessing.

Furthermore, even with the best of intentions, deception is deception. I [Costi] have a former colleague in the faith-healing circuit who is fully convinced (and ok with it) that many of the healings claimed in his meetings are faked and claimed by people who want to be prayed for on the platform. Claiming you were healed is one of the best ways to make it on stage at a healing crusade—if not the only way.

His answer when I asked him why he doesn't quit going along with the charade and just offer people truth? He says that it's not his job to focus on who is or isn't lying. He believes his job is to give people hope and increase their faith so they can activate their healing that Christ already paid for in the atonement. If he can do that by being optimistic about even the potentially false healings, then that is fulfilling his calling in his mind.

This category fits Paul's exact words to Timothy about the contrast between those who will be faithful to the boundaries of God's Word, and those who will irreverently or ignorantly do things as they please:

> But evil men and impostors will proceed from bad to worse, deceiving and being deceived. You, however, continue in the things you have learned and become convinced of, knowing from whom you have learned them, and that from childhood you have known the sacred writings which are able to give you the wisdom that leads to salvation through faith which is in Christ Jesus. All Scripture is inspired by God and profitable for teaching, for reproof, for correction, for training in righteousness; so that the man of God may be adequate, equipped for every good work. (2 Tim 3:13–17)

None of these scenarios negates that a sovereign God can will and work in the life of one of His sheep at any given time. If a person is in fact a genuine believer, he or she will not stay in a false church long-term, and he or she will be malleable to God's Word as it informs previous experiences under a false teacher.

There is nothing wrong with a Christian praising God for being healed by the Great Physician or his or her medical doctor, but there is something dangerous about an enthusiastic perspective that believes a false teacher is just a well-meaning (though somewhat mistaken) healer who did the healing. We cannot stand idle while sheep are left untaught.

Experience never defines biblical truth. The truth found in Scripture must always define our experience.

Selected Bibliography

Armstrong, John H. *The Coming Evangelical Crisis: Current Challenges to the Authority of Scripture and the Gospel*. Chicago, IL: Moody Press, 1996.

Artman, Amy Collier. "Protecting Her Image: Kathryn Kuhlman and the Manipulation of Negation." *Bulletin for the Study of Religion* 43, no. 2 (April 2014): 1–23.

Barrett, David B., George T. Kurian, and Todd M. Johnson, eds. *World Christian Encyclopedia*. 2nd ed. 2 vols. New York: Oxford University Press, 2001.

Beeke, Joel. "Calvin's Piety." *Mid-America Journal of Theology* 15 (2004): 33–65. Accessed December 15, 2017. http://www.midamerica .edu/uploads/files/pdf/journal/15-beekepiety.pdf.

Berkhof, Louis. *Systematic Theology*. Grand Rapids, MI: Eerdmans, 1965.

Bowler, Kate. *Blessed: A History of the American Prosperity Gospel*. New York: Oxford University Press, 2013.

Brown, Colin, ed. *The New International Dictionary of New Testament Theology*. 4 vols. Grand Rapids, MI: Zondervan 1986.

Buckingham, Jamie. *Daughter of Destiny: The Only Authorized Biography of Kathryn Kuhlman*. Alachua, FL: Bridge Logos, 2008.

Burgess, Stanley M., Gary B. McGee, and Patrick H. Alexander, eds. *Dictionary of Pentecostal and Charismatic Movements*. Grand Rapids, MI: Zondervan, 1988.

Clark, William Newton. *An Outline of Christian Theology*. New York: Scribner, 1901.

Coleman, Simon. *The Globalization of Charismatic Christianity*. Cambridge, UK: Cambridge University Press, 2000.

Collins, John, and Peter M. Duyzer. "The Intersection of William Bran-ham and Jim Jones." Alternative Considerations of Jonestown & Peoples Temple. Last modified October 20, 2014. Accessed Nov-ember 20, 2016. http://jonestown.sdsu.edu/?page_id=61481.

Craig, Philip A. "'And Prophecy Shall Cease': Jonathan Edwards on the Cessation of the Gift of Prophecy." *Westminster Theological Journal* 64, no. 1 (2002): 163–184.

Douglas, James. "The Divine Immanency." *Bibliotheca Sacra* 45, no. 180 (1888): 567–584.

Edgar, Thomas R. *Miraculous Gifts: Are They For Today?* Neptune, NJ: Loizeaux Brothers, 1983.

Erasmus, Desiderius. *The Praise of Folly.* Edited and translated by Hoyt H. Hudson. Princeton, NJ: Princeton University Press, 1970.

Erickson, Millard. *Christian Theology.* 2nd ed. Grand Rapids, MI: Baker Books, 1998.

Erickson, Millard, Paul Kjoss Helseth, and Justin Taylor, eds. *Reclaiming the Center: Confronting Evangelical Accommodation in Postmodern Times.* Wheaton, IL: Crossway, 2004.

Fisher, Richard, and Kurt Goedelman. *The Confusing World of Benny Hinn.* St. Louis, MO: Personal Freedom Outreach, 2013.

Goff, James R., Jr. *Fields White Unto Harvest: Charles F. Parham and the Missionary Origins of Pentecostalism.* Fayetteville, AR: University of Arkansas Press, 1988.

Grudem, Wayne. *The Gift of Prophecy in the New Testament and Today.* Westchester, IL: Crossway, 1988.

——. *Systematic Theology: An Introduction to Biblical Doctrine.* Grand Rapids, MI: Zondervan, 1994.

Gundry, Robert H. "Ecstatic Utterance (N.E.B.)." *Journal of Theological Studies* 17, no. 2 (October 1966): 299–307.

Hagin, Kenneth. *I Went to Hell.* Tulsa, OK: K. Hagin Ministries, 1982.

——. *Zoe: The God Kind of Life*. Tulsa, OK: Kenneth Hagin Ministries, 1989.

Hagin, Kenneth. *The Name of Jesus*. Tulsa, OK: Kenneth Hagin Ministries, 2007.

Hall, Franklin. *Atomic Power With God: Through Prayer and Fasting*. San Diego, CA: Franklin Hall, 1946. Accessed December 10, 2017. http://standsure.net/books/hall.htm

Hanley, P. J. *They Call Themselves Apostle: How Revival Churches Have Been Hijacked by the New Apostolic Reformation*. CreateSpace, 2017.

Hawkins, Greg L., and Cally Parkinson. *Move: What 1,000 Churches Reveal About Spiritual Growth*. Grand Rapids, MI: Zondervan, 2011.

Hazlitt, William, trans. *The Table Talk of Martin Luther* (London: H. G. Bohn, 1857.

Hollenweger, Walter J. *Pentecostalism: Origins and Developments Worldwide*. Peabody, MA: Hendrickson Publishers, 1997.

Hunt, Stephen. "Deliverance: The Evolution of a Doctrine." *Themelios* 21, no. 1 (1995): 10–13.

Hyatt, Eddie L. *2000 Years of Charismatic History*. Lake Mary, FL: Charisma House, 2002.

Jensen, Peter F. "Calvin, Charismatics and Miracles." *Evangelical Quarterly* 51, no. 3 (1979), 131–144.

Johnson, Bill. *Releasing the Spirit of Prophecy: The Supernatural Power of Testimony*. Shippensburg, PA: Destiny Image, 2014.

——. *The Supernatural Power of a Transformed Mind: Access to a Life of Miracles*. Shippensburg, PA: Destiny Image, 2005.

——. *When Heaven Invades Earth: A Practical Guide to a Life of Miracles*. Shippensburg, PA: Destiny Image, 2003.

Johnson, Phillip. "Rubber Prophecies." Pyromaniac Blog. Posted November 4, 2005. Accessed December 23, 2016. http://phillip johnson.blogspot.com/2005/11/rubber-prophecies.html

Jones, David W., and Russell S. Woodbridge. *Health, Wealth, and Happiness: Has the Prosperity Gospel Overshadowed the Gospel of Christ?* Grand Rapids, MI: Kregel Publications, 2011.

Keener, Craig S. *Acts: An Exegetical Commentary.* 3 vols. Grand Rapids, MI: Baker Academic, 2012.

———. "Spirit Possession as a Cross-Cultural Experience." *Bulletin for Biblical Research* 20, no. 2 (2010): 215–235.

Kent, Homer. *The Epistle to the Hebrews.* Grand Rapids, MI: Baker Book House, 1972.

Liardon, Roberts. *God's Generals: Why They Succeeded and Why Some Failed.* New Kensington, PA: Whitaker House, 1996.

MacArthur, John. "Does God Do Miracles Today?" Grace To You, August 11, 1991. Accessed August 03, 2017. https://www.gty.org/library/sermons-library/90-56/does-god-do-miracles-today.

———. *1 Corinthians.* MacArthur New Testament Commentary. Chicago: Moody Press, 1984.

———. *Hebrews.* MacArthur New Testament Commentary. Chicago, IL: Moody Publishers, 1983.

MacArthur, John, and Richard Mayhue, eds. *Biblical Doctrine: A Systematic Summary of Bible Truth.* Wheaton, IL: Crossway, 2017.

McConnell, D. R. *A Different Gospel: A Historical and Biblical Analysis of the Modern Faith Movement.* Rev. ed. Peabody, MA: Hendrickson Publishers, 1995.

Miller, J. R. *Elders Lead a Healthy Family: Shared Leadership for a Vibrant Church.* Eugene, OR: Wipf and Stock Publishers, 2017.

———. *Have You Not Yet Received the Spirit?: Finding Unity through the Baptism in the Holy Spirit.* San Diego, CA: Emerging Life Resources, 2008.

———. *Promise of the Father: Healing the Christian Legacy of Segregation and Denominationalism.* Puyallup, WA: Emerging Life Resources, 2008.

Moore, Richard P. *Divergent Theology: An Inquiry Into the Theological Char-acteristics of the Word of Faith Third Wave Movement and The New Apo-stolic Reformation.* CreateSpace, 2017.

Newman, Scott. "The Appeal of God's Truth to the Mind: Theological and Exegetical Answers to Post-Modern Trends within Evangelical Thought." *Conservative Theological Journal* 1, no. 2 (1997): 140–162.

Noll, Mark. *The New Shape of World Christianity: How American Experience Reflects Global Faith.* Downers Grove, IL: Intervarsity Press, 2009.

"Oral and Evelyn Roberts." Richard Roberts, Oral Roberts Ministries. Accessed December 23, 2016. http://oralroberts.com/about/our-history/oral-roberts/.

Packer, J. I. *Keep in Step with the Spirit: Finding Fullness in our Walk With God.* Grand Rapids, MI: Baker Books, 2005.

Parham, Charles. *A Voice Crying In The Wilderness.* 1902. Reprint, Baxter Springs, KS: Parham, 1944.

Parham, Sarah. *The Life of Charles F. Parham.* Joplin, MO: Hunter Printing, 1930.

Payne, J. Barton. *Encyclopedia of Biblical Prophecy.* Grand Rapids, MI: Ba-ker Books, 1980.

"Pentecost Has Come: The Apostolic Faith Movement," *The Apostolic Faith* 1, no. 1 (September 1906): 2–4. Accessed January 9, 2018. http://apostolicfaith.org/library/historical/azusa-originals/Azusa-Paper-Original-01.pdf.

Promised Restoration website. http://www.en.branham.ru/index.php.

"A Prophetic Message, Given by Mrs. R. J. Semple, in Belfast, Ireland While en Route to China." *Pentecostal Testimony* 1, no. 5 (July 1, 1910), 1–16. Accessed December 7, 2017. http://ifphc.org/Digital Publications/USA/Independent/Pentecostal%20Testimony/Unregistered/1910/FPHC/1910_07.pdf.

Randall, John Herman. *Making of the Modern Mind: A Survey of the Intellectual Background of the Present Age.* Boston: Houghton Mifflin, 1940.

The Revival Alliance website. http://revivalalliance.com.

Roberts, Oral. *If You Need Healing Do These Things.* Garden City, NY: Country Life Press, 1950.

Ruthven, Jon Mark. *On the Cessation of the Charismata.* Tulsa, OK: Word & Spirit Press, 2011.

Sartre, Jean-Paul. *Being and Nothingness: An Essay on Phenomenological Ontology.* New York: Philosophical Library, 1956.

Shelley, Bruce. *Church History in Plain Language.* 4th ed. Nashville, TN: Thomas Nelson, 2013.

Snoeberger, Mark A. "Tongues—Are They for Today?" *Detroit Baptist Seminary Journal* 14 (2009): 3–21

Simmons, Dale H. *E. W. Kenyon and the Postbellum Pursuit of Peace, Power, and Plenty.* Lanham, MD: Scarecrow, 1997.

Strachan, C. Gordon. *The Pentecostal Theology of Edward Irving.* Peabody, MA: Hendrickson, 1973.

Sutton, Matthew A. *Aimee Semple McPherson and the Resurrection of Christian America.* Cambridge, MA: Harvard University Press, 2007. Accessed October 14, 2016. eBook Academic Collection, EBSCOhost.

Synan, Vinson, ed. *The Century of the Holy Spirit: 100 Years of Pentecostal and Charismatic Renewal, 1901–2001.* Nashville: Thomas Nelson, 2001.

Thomas, Keith. *Religion and the Decline of Magic.* London: Oxford University Press, 1971.

Tozer, A. W. *The Knowledge of the Holy: The Attributes Of God, Their Meaning In The Christian Life.* New York: Harper & Row, 1961.

Unger, Frederick Merrill. "The Baptism with the Holy Spirit Part 3" *Bibliotheca Sacra* 101, no. 404 (October 1944): 486–88.

Wagner, C. Peter. *The Changing Church*. Ventura, CA: Gospel Light, 2004.

———. *Spheres of Authority: Apostles in Today's Church*. Wagner Publications, 2002.

Warfield, Benjamin B. *Counterfeit Miracles*. New York, NY: Charles Scribner's Sons, 1918.

Weaver, C. Douglas. *The Healer-Prophet, William Marrion Branham: A Study of the Prophetic in American Pentecostalism*. Macon, GA: Mercer University Press, 1987.

Whyte, H. A. Maxwell. "A Body Thou Prepared Me." *New Wine Magazine* 1, no. 3 (November 1969): 1, 5-6. Accessed December 12, 2017. https://csmpublishing.org/wp-content/NewWineArchives/Full_Issues/1969/NewWineMagazine_Issue_11-1969.pdf

Wiersbe, Warren W. *The Bible Exposition Commentary: New Testament*. 2nd ed. Colorado Springs, CO: David C. Cook, 2008.

Wigglesworth, Smith. *Ever Increasing Faith*. Springfield, MO: Gospel Publishing House, 1924.

Wildberger, Hans. *Isaiah 13–27 A Continental Commentary*. Minneapolis, MN: Fortress Press, 1997.

Wilson, Julian. *Wigglesworth: The Complete Story*. Tyrone, GA: Authentic Media, 2004.

Wimber, John, and Kevin Springer. *Power Healing*. San Francisco, CA: Harper & Row, 1987.

81037825R00113

Made in the USA
Middletown, DE
19 July 2018